A Eulogy for Capitalism

A Eulogy for Capitalism
and Other Essays, 1998-2016

James Herod

Boston
2018

*A Eulogy for Capitalism
and Other Essays, 1998-2016*

© 2018 by James Herod

Published by the Lantern Library
https://thelanternlibrary.wordpress.com

ISBN: **978-0-9983797-4-6**

Type set in 12 point Schoolbook.
6" x 9", 201 pages

Book and Cover design by Rosalie Montenigro

More of the author's work can be found at:
www.jamesherod.info

Cover photographs were taken from a video of the 2013 Funeral March for Capitalism in Boston, which was filmed by the author.

Contents

Preface 7

1 A Eulogy for Capitalism 15
2 Capitalists, Global Warming, and the Climate Justice Movement.. 19
3 Is Greed All That is Wrong with Capitalism? 41
4 A Stake, Not a Mistake: On Not Seeing the Enemy.... 61
5 Abolish the Stock Market 85
6 May Day Talk 93
7 The Loss of Anti-Capitalism 97
8 A Great History of Capitalism 107
9 A Leninist Loooks at Venezuela............................ 113
10 Peter Gelderloos Visits Boston 123
11 *Sicko*, a Review of Michael Moore's Film of 2007 .. 129
12 Sketch of an Anarchist Revolutionary Strategy.... 135
13 Consolidation of Fascism, American Style 139
14 Capitalism and Transportation Infrastructure 155
15 A Response to a Letter by Paul M. Weyrich.......... 161
16 Indigenism: A Critique 175
17 Defeating Capitalists Quickly to Save the Earth ... 189

Preface

James Herod, October 2018, Boston

To speak of a eulogy for Capitalism is premature maybe, a bit, you think? We can hope of course. But is it hope or a pipedream? In Boston, on May Day in 2012 and again in 2013, anarchists organized a Funeral March for Capitalism. These events were a lot of fun, with puppets galore, some floats, a marching band, all kinds of neat costumes, and hundreds of us marching through downtown Boston. For the second one the organizers wanted a Eulogy for Capitalism, to be delivered by a pretend capitalist, to use at the rally which launched the march. So I wrote the one included here. The organizers decided to go with a much shorter, funnier one, in which the capitalist was made to apologize and grovel. Indeed, it is hard to imagine my entry being read to a rally of hundreds on the Boston Commons. But I've always liked it, even if it wasn't appropriate for the occasion.

But is it going to happen, in time that is, before capitalists destroy the earth and kill us all? Is humankind going to be rid of capitalists before global warming (which is caused by capitalists) has melted the arctic, which will release hundreds or even thousands of gigatons of methane, which will poison the atmosphere and acidify the oceans, rendering all life on earth untenable? I'm pretty much convinced that we will not. A few climate scientists say it is already too late (as of 2018); there is enough carbon dioxide in the atmosphere right now to melt the arctic. A

Venus like atmosphere could happen within three, or four, or five decades, they say. If that happens we will be needing a Eulogy for the Living Earth, except that there will be no one to write it. The evidence for this prognosis of the Near Term Extinction of earth life, including humankind, seems to be mounting rapidly, substantially, and alarmingly. I can only hope to high heaven that the prognosis is wrong.

It seems that we may have run out of time to defeat capitalists. Their social order, based on the accumulation of capital for its own sake, and which elevates this practice above the survival of life itself, has proved too resilient and powerful, and for over five hundred years has overcome all resistance to it. This capitalist social order is now global in scope, is deeply entrenched, and permeates virtually every country. It is massive. Huge cities everywhere. Landscapes transformed. Local self-sufficiency destroyed. Forests destroyed. Commodification of everything. Market forces prevailing globally, with the social relations of seven billion people increasingly being organized around the capitalists' drive to keep accumulating more capital, to keep "growing," to keep the profits flowing in, and to keep anti-capitalists at bay, even if it means destroying whole countries, and war, endless war.

There might be a solution to global warming even now. If humankind could shift rapidly to sustainable organic agriculture, this could begin to remove carbon dioxide from the atmosphere, especially if this were combined with a massive, global reforestation program, and a rapid conversion to clean energy sources and away from oil, coal, and gas. Other ways have been proposed for cooling the earth. But how are we going to get these global campaigns? We would have to defeat the extremely rich and powerful fossil fuel corporations, agribusiness, and also the market forces driving deforestation, like the demands for lumber, palm oil, and beef, among other things. Most every government in the world would have to endorse and support these programs. Yet most governments are largely controlled by capitalists, and so they defend and support the corporations that are destroying the earth. It is difficult to see how such globally entrenched power could be unseated. It will certainly take a lot more than protest marches and rallies at the annual United Nations' Conference of the Parties (COP). Nevertheless, in a companion volume to this one, *Engaging Anarchism: Selected Papers, 1999-2014*, I try to grapple with issues of revolutionary strategy, with how to defeat capitalists, although now our task is how to defeat them quickly. As for that, I have included here an essay from December 2016 in which I outline some strategy proposals for attacking money as part of our struggle to more quickly overthrow capitalism.

I have included here a paper on the global warming crisis which I wrote after the COP15 conference in Copenhagen in 2009. It has a grim ending, in which I claim that "Our only option now is Anarchy or Death." But this claim is realistic I think. It would take a massive, global, anti-capitalist movement to stop and reverse the capitalist social order from inadvertently extinguishing life on earth through its unrelenting drive for profit above all else. It would take a miracle for such a movement to emerge. But miracles sometimes happen; that is, history is full of surprises. Maybe enough hundreds of millions of people will wake up in time to recognize their enemies – capitalists and their states – and deal with them and thus save themselves and the earth. There are some indications that a transformation in world consciousness may be underway. This is our only hope.

Most of the essays included in this volume are about capitalism in one way or another, but most were written before I became fully aware of the extreme seriousness and direness of the global warming crisis that we face. Even so, they are still useful for helping us to understand capitalism, which is essential for us to do if we are to build a global anti-capitalist movement. As for what comes after capitalism, anarchy is the best choice, hands down. Peter Gelderloos' book, *Anarchy Works* (reviewed here), envisions what it might look like. As for getting out of capitalism and into anarchy, I've outlined a suggested approach in my book *Getting Free*, and many of the papers in my book *Engaging Anarchism* deal with strategy. But for this collection, I've just included a sketch of an anarchist strategy (No. 12).

The essay on greed is just as relevant today as it was nineteen years ago in **1999**. The habit of blaming our woes on the greed of capitalists, rather than on the dynamics of the capitalist system itself, is well nigh universal in the so-called alternative or progressive media. The obvious implication is that ungreedy capitalists would be okay. Only a small minority of Marxist and anarchist writers, who are sorely marginalized and relatively unknown, condemn capitalism per se. To get an understanding of the internal dynamics of the capitalist social order, everyone should read Immanuel Wallerstein's little masterpiece, *Historical Capitalism*. That will cure you of thinking that if only capitalists weren't so greedy we wouldn't be in such dire straits.

I took the title of the essay, "A Stake, Not a Mistake," from an article of the same name which I helped write in **1969**. Several of us in the Committee of Returned Volunteers had made up a broadsheet (an 11 x 17 printed sheet, folded into an 8-1/2 x 11 handout) which we distributed in the hundreds at the big anti-war demonstration in Washington, DC in November of that year. The idea that the US war against Vietnam was a mistake was quite prevalent at that time even amongst anti-war activists. We sought to counter that notion by documenting how the war served the purposes of US imperialism.

So here it is forty-nine years later, and the claim that US foreign policy is a mistake, a failure, a disaster, is just everywhere, all across the alternative, progressive, left-liberal media, just as in the case of greed. This shows, disheartingly, how capitalism is still seriously misunderstood even by the majority of today's dissidents and pro-

Preface

testers. In reality, the United States of America, since its inception in 1789, has determinedly pursued a consistent foreign policy with one overriding objective: to make the world safe for American capitalists. It has been enormously successful. The cases cited in my essay could be augmented a hundred times over.

For example, it is almost universally believed today that the United States was defeated in Vietnam. This is not true. The US won that war. It accomplished all its major objectives. It destroyed the possibility of an independent Vietnam, and in the process demolished two other countries – Cambodia and Laos – and thus prevented Southeast Asia from ever escaping the orbit of US imperialism. The US attack on Vietnam also created the conditions for the US/CIA-engineered destruction of the Indonesian communist party through the mass murder of around a million partisans in 1965-66, leading to the overthrow of Indonesian anti-imperialist president, Sukarno, in 1967, and the installation of the US puppet, Suharto, who would rule that nation of 105 million (203 million by 1998) for the next 31 years, until 1998. As for Vietnam itself, today it is one of the most rabidly capitalist countries in the world. Southeast Asia as a whole – Vietnam, Cambodia, Laos, Thailand, Malaysia, Singapore, Indonesia, Myanmar, Philippines – is now a capitalist powerhouse. The persistent and prevailing myth that the US was defeated in Vietnam is one of the most strikingly successful propaganda coups of the past half century.

During the past two decades the United States has broken up and largely destroyed six independent nations – Yugoslavia, Afghanistan, Iraq, Libya, Somalia, and Yemen. We should also include Palestine. Now it is working on Syria (and hungrily eyeing Iran). That makes eight (soon to be nine?). So what do we hear from our "progressives"? They are alarmed because US foreign policy is such a disaster, and is creating all this chaos, mayhem, poverty, up-rootedness, wretchedness, broken families, disease, homelessness, forced migration, and death. My God! What would it take to convince these people that the United States does all this on purpose, even if it means a financial loss for the empire, in order to continue to make the world safe for capitalism, and prevent the emergence of an alternative? When a superpower bombs a country's water, sewage, and electrical systems, its hospitals, schools, libraries, and museums, its governmental buildings, the residences of its leaders, its airports, highways, railroads, bridges, and ports, its food warehouses and fuel storage facilities, its trains and ships, not to mention its army, navy, and air force, but not its oil fields (!), how could anyone think that this was not deliberate? But they do. You see it every day, incessantly, in the writings of the commentariat, progressive and otherwise.

Yet, it might be that the smoke screen protecting capitalism is beginning to thin a bit, or even to dissipate. The savagery of its criminal attacks and destruction is just so damned blatant, and is done so openly and brazenly, that it gets harder and harder for people not to realize that it is intentional. This is especially true for populations outside the core capitalist countries, who have a first-hand and personal understanding of imperialism anyway, having lived under its onerous yoke for so many centuries. But perhaps consciousness is beginning to change also in the core capitalist countries. I certainly hope so.

My brief article on "Abolishing the Stock Market" was written in response to the international financial meltdown of 2007-2008. But I had been honing in on money for some time, as a neglected but significant topic, which should be included in any strategy proposals for defeating capitalists, especially since I attended a conference on money in 2004. A written response to that conference, as well as a bibliography on money which I have compiled, are included in my *Engaging Anarchism* collection.

My essay on "The Loss of Anti-Capitalism" was written about a year and a half before a new, resurgent radical movement burst into the political arena in November 1999 in Seattle. I had not been aware that such a movement had been building. For me 1998 was still in the pits of the counterrevolution that had dominated American political life since the early 1970s. And I think I'm correct in saying that even at that late date (thirty years after the defeat of the revolutionary movements of the 1960s) it was still next to impossible to even mention the words capitalism and imperialism, so thoroughly had the left been suppressed and silenced. On this matter, I'm happy to say that the situation has changed rather dramatically in the past eighteen years. These new 21st century radicals, with anarchists numbering significantly in their ranks, began as staunch anti-capitalists and anti-imperialists. Globally, capitalism has finally come back under critical scrutiny, like it was in the late 19th and early 20th centuries. It is becoming harder and harder for millions of people not to connect the dots, between capitalism and global warming, for example, or between the imposed austerity, or the financial crises, or the dismembering and destruction of whole countries, and capitalism. Neoliberal capitalism is capitalism stripped of its ideological veneer. It stands naked before the world. Its crimes are exposed openly for all to see. But there is still a long way to go. Many more millions of people worldwide must connect the dots, if we are to have a chance to survive and to try again to establish a just and free society.

Since I wrote the article on fascism in 2004 things have gotten much, much worse, dramatically worse. I didn't continue working on this topic. Many others have been doing a fine job of documenting the loss of our liberties, and the country's rapid slide towards full-fledged fascism.

My critique of indigenism was an attempt to counter a fairly widespread conceptual framework which leaves class out of the picture, or even explicitly rejects it, when analyzing current political affairs. It is basically a form of identity politics. The other essays included here are pretty much self-explanatory.

1
A Eulogy for Capitalism

*The following text was written, but not used, for the 2013 May Day **Funeral March for Capitalism**, in Boston – a wonderful, festive, fun event.*

*L*adies and Gentlemen,
My name is Gimme Moneysucker. I am the former CEO of Bank of America. I also previously worked for Goldman Sachs and JP Morgan. I was in and out of the US Treasury Department for decades. I've served on the Boards of Directors of several of America's most wonderful businesses – ExxonMobil, Monsanto, and Raytheon. I used to live in a beautiful ten million dollar townhouse right over there on Beacon Hill. I had in-house gourmet cooks, and an abundance of Haitian servants. Now that's all gone. The house was confiscated, along with my classic art collection, and everything else. I've also lost my get-away retreat on Saint Kitts, and my far-away vacation home in Bora Bora. Not to mention my private jet. So it is a sad day for me personally, but sadder still that the ingenious scheme of theft that made me rich is here no more – just because of you scumbags and losers standing here today. I'm surprised you even invited me to give this eulogy. Or lament, actually. Well, I suppose it is better than the guillotine. But it's your mistake, you dumb fucks. We'll be back.
 We capitalists had a very good run – 500 years of

Chapter 1

extremely profitable fleecing, swindling, conning, and just plain stealing. Not without opposition, of course, but nothing we couldn't handle. Those peasant revolts in the sixteenth century weren't much bother. We simply told them that their land was ours, and drove them off into the cities where they had to hire out to our factory bosses. Natives put up a bit of a fight. But we had sailing ships with cannons, and horses and swords, and later muskets. It's true we had to kill about 50 million of those damn savages to conquer the Americas. But my god it was worth it! The gold and silver just came pouring in. And after the gold ran out we had sugar and cotton. Lily-livered moralists keep complaining that we killed fifteen million black slaves in the Atlantic Crossing alone. But who gave a damn? Those plantations were worth a fortune, gold mines in themselves.

Communists weren't hard to neutralize and derail. Lenin was the best thing that could have happened to our capitalist class. The Soviet Union was the perfect enemy. It was just capitalism in another guise, but almost no one realized that. But we knew, and knew also that they couldn't run a country, and were messing up big time, mismanaging. Then when the whole Soviet empire suddenly went poof and vanished from history overnight, we went in and stripped the country clean, making off with trillions, all the while claiming that we had won. What a windfall that was! Plus we were able to set up a textbook case of mafia capitalism. A wet dream come true.

Socialists, naïve gullible socialists, had this foolish idea that they could get rid of us by winning elections and packing our parliaments with their buddies. So we were willing to play this silly game with them for over a century, all the while we were raking in the profits and building up our forces. They never came even close to weakening us. Eventually, though, we got bored with the ritual and simply took over the governments ourselves.

Anarchists were never a threat at all. In that little skirmish in Chicago in the 1880s we simply rounded up a bunch of them and hung or jailed them, or drove them to suicide. That was the end of that. Spain was a bit of a problem, but we were able to use the communists to kill the anarchists, so we came out of that on top, with a good strong dictator to run capitalism there for another half century.

Strikes? We just waited them out. Factory occupations? Picked them off one by one. Mass demonstrations? Great! They didn't hurt us at all. They were very amusing, big jokes, in fact. We were dying laughing.

So that's how it has gone, for five hundred years, with us getting richer and richer, and with you miserable slobs, the despicable multitude – weak, gullible, stupid –just groveling, whining, complaining, protesting but never really fighting and never winning. What pathetic creatures, a sweating swarm of humanity begging to be enslaved.

Recently we destroyed Yugoslavia, Afghanistan, Iraq, and Libya, and we were working on Somali and Yemen, and would soon have destroyed Syria, all without a whimper from the ever acquiescing masses. Wars were one of our greatest sources of profit, a never-ending bonanza. We not only enriched ourselves by selling governments all those planes, tanks, and ships, but we also raked in millions in interest on the loans we gave to governments to wage the wars. It was a sweetheart deal. It's a shame the racket has been busted up.

I can't help but gloat over one of our most spectacular scams run just recently. We got the US Treasury to give us 23 trillion dollars to cover our gambling debts, and at the same time made sure that not even one dollar would go to help the foreclosed homeowners. Now our banks are gobbling up those houses for pennies on the dollar. Was there a revolution? An insurrection even? A big protest at least? No. Nothing. So I thought, "We're home free." We capitalists are set for another hundred years.

But then the damned popular assemblies started springing up. First in Greece in 2008 in Snytagma square. Then from that awful mob in Tahrir Square in Egypt. We had seen a few of these before, in Algeria, Argentina, Bolivia, and Mexico, but they quickly passed and we weren't too worried. But then suddenly on March 15, 2012 in Spain, assemblies were everywhere, in every public square across the entire nation. This was a bit more worrisome, especially because they rejected all political parties and unions and didn't even think of trying to seize power. Finally, and to our utter consternation, there was a blasted popular assembly right smack on our doorstep in Wall Street, across the street from the Stock Exchange, which lasted for weeks. And it was pointing the finger at us, the 1%, the people who know how to make money off money. We rule the world, for Christ's Sake! Then, even worse, there were assemblies in a thousand towns across America. People of the world cheered, that finally there was a show of resistance in the heart of the empire, they said. Our hearts sank.

And so began our unraveling. To our great surprise, the 99% began to catch on to our scam. I guess it was the brutal austerity which we were imposing that was the tipping point. The rip-off was just too blatant. They also claimed that we were destroying the earth, without blinking an eye, in order to keep our profits rolling in. This was balderdash, of course, but they believed it. So this too might have had something to do with our demise.

But don't you worry. We will be back. We will find a new way to exploit and enslave you. Humans are a sorry lot, all around. You won't succeed in setting up this pipe dream of yours – a world full of democratic autonomous communities, you say, based on equality, freedom, justice. Fat chance. So, enjoy your pitiful little Funeral March for Capitalism. I hate your guts, all of you.

2
Capitalists, Global Warming, and the Climate Justice Movement

*[Prefatory Note: The first part of this essay was originally written in December 2009 for the monthly **Newsletter** of the Boston Anti-Authoritarian Movement, #29, January 2010. A substantial postscript, from May 2010, continues the discussion.*

For the purposes of this essay I will assume that the science which establishes that the earth is warming up is correct. This is what all participants to the COP15 conference believed, both inside the conference hall and outside in the streets. For a brief note on dissenting views, see Footnote No. 4.

*This essay was also published in the **Anarcho-Syndicalist Review**, #54, Summer 2010, pages 23-28. For this edition of the work, I've made a few more (17) changes and additions. I also restored some page numbers in the bibliography, and a few full URLs, which had been dropped in the magazine edition to save space. The essay is posted on my website <http://www.jamesherod.info> under Selected Papers 1998 to Present.]*

Chapter 2

The fifteenth meeting of the Conference of Participants (COP15) in the Kyoto Protocol took place this month in Copenhagen, Denmark from December 7 to 18, 2009. The purpose of the conference was to wrap up more than two years of negotiations by representatives of all the world's governments to get a legally binding treaty for a new round of reductions in carbon emissions under the UN's Kyoto Protocol to replace the first round which was expiring.

So, what happened? The United States sabotaged the negotiations by refusing to agree to any legally binding treaty, by refusing to commit itself to any significant reduction of its own carbon pollution, and by refusing to work through the UN's open and democratic negotiating process, instead maneuvering behind the scenes in secret to strike a deal with a few select countries which was then sprung on the conference at the last minute. Naturally, the negotiations collapsed and the conference ended in failure, except for the United States, for whom the outcome is obviously what it had intended all along. To understand the significance and probable consequences of this event some background will be necessary.

Amidst growing reports from the world's climatologists of alarming increases in temperatures worldwide due to increased levels of carbon dioxide in the atmosphere, a treaty was fashioned at the Earth Summit in Rio de Janeiro, Brazil, in 1992, called the United Nations Framework Convention on Climate Change. To date, 192 nations have signed the treaty. The United States tried to obstruct this summit from its outset. The original draft of the treaty had to be greatly weakened and watered down before the United States would agree to sign on.

The same thing happened five years later in Kyoto, Japan, in 1997, where an addition to the Rio treaty was being negotiated to put some teeth into it through legally binding cuts in carbon emissions. Once again, the United States was obstructive, refusing to cooperate, unless reductions in carbon emissions were handled through the market (the so-called "Cap and Trade, with Offsets"). Al Gore flew to Kyoto to negotiate this demand. The world finally agreed, just in order to get some treaty, but then the US never ratified the Kyoto Protocol anyway.

Gore's presence at this crucial conference is significant. He had been for some time closely involved with Wall Street's efforts to create a market for carbon trading. In a brilliantly researched essay.[1] David Noble persuasively argues that there had been a split in the capitalist ruling class with regard to global warming. Their original response (and propaganda) was to deny it. But then the financial elite realized that a lot of money could be made if carbon emissions could be commoditized and traded on the market. They launched a massive propaganda campaign to convince the world that global warming was real, that it was being caused by humans (by burning fossil fuels), and that capitalists could solve the problem through their normal market mechanisms. Global warming moved into the mainstream.

The purpose of the Kyoto Protocol was to reduce carbon emissions and thus cool the earth. The purpose of Wall Street is to make money. So far, Wall Street has prevailed, as was demonstrated again in December in Copenhagen. Twelve years after the Kyoto Protocol was signed in 1997 it is clear that the market approach, insisted on by the United States, has not worked. Carbon emissions have not declined in most countries. They have increased. Most climate justice activists totally reject Wall Street's scheme. They have produced detailed, empirical studies to prove

---

1 David F. Noble, "The Corporate Climate Coup," posted on Global Research website on May 4, 2007. <http://www.globalresearch.ca/PrintArticle.php?articleId=5568>. I have since learned that David Noble doesn't believe in global warming, mainly because he doesn't trust peer reviewed science. It is a weird, and I believe mistaken, position, at least for the case of global warming. See "Peer Review as Censorship: An Interview with David Noble," by Suzan Mazur. Posted on *Counterpunch* on the weekend edition for February 26-28, 2010, at: <http://www.counterpunch.org/mazur02262010.html>.

Chapter 2

that it hasn't worked.[2]

Yet we are in an extremely harsh time frame on this problem. If the science is correct, very substantial reductions in carbon emissions worldwide must be achieved in the next ten years, with the nearly total elimination of fossil fuels within the next twenty to thirty years. If the 2020 goals are not met, there is the danger that a tipping point will be reached, setting in motion irreversible warming trends, with the release of billions of tons of methane gas presently trapped in the frozen tundra stretching across northern Canada and Siberia, and billions more tons trapped in nodules deep in the oceans, the loss of the oceans as a carbon sink as they become acidified, and the loss of reflected heat with the melting of the polar ice caps, glaciers, and Greenland's ice. The earth will become unrecognizable, and all life on it will be threatened.

What are the chances that the United States will change its policy anytime soon, in time to help stave off the tipping point? Virtually zero. Corporate control, especially by Wall Street and Big Oil, over the United States government is now nearly total, and is irreversible within existing institutional structures. The 40-year-old counter-revolution by neoconservative free market ideologues to make sure that corporate control was never threatened again, as

---

[2] See for example Tamra Gilbertson and Oscar Reyes, *Carbon Trading: How It Works and Why It Fails* (Critical Currents, No. 7, November 2009). There is a rare (on the left) dissenting view about "Cap and Trade" by the well-known radical scholar Robin Hahnel. He believes that Cap and Trade could work if a few changes were made in the system, and he believes the left should support this because whether we like it or not the world is presently organized through the market and is likely to remain so for some time. So this is our best chance to get carbon emissions reduced, he argues. See his three part-essay on "The Left and Climate Change" posted on Znet on December 24-26, 2009 at: http://www.zcommunications.org/zspace/viewCommentaryPrint/4806>, <...4087>, <...4088>.

By the way, there is a competing mainstream proposal to Cap and Trade, namely, Fee and Dividend. This proposal is supported by James Hansen, one of the first scientists to raise the alarm about global warming. He is the director of NASA's Goddard Institute of Space Studies. For a description of the proposal see James Hansen, "Cap and Fade," at: <http://www.commondreams.org/prnt/50274>.

it had been in the sixties, has been completely successful. It would take a revolution to reverse this, and there is no sign anywhere of that happening, certainly not in time.

Perhaps the other 191 nations in the treaty could just go ahead without the United States? Perhaps. But they could have (and should have) done that in Rio in 1992. Why didn't they? Why was the treaty watered down to accommodate the United States? They certainly should have gone ahead without the US in Kyoto. Why did they cave in to US demands for "Cap and Trade"? They most certainly should have done so this month in Copenhagen. But they didn't. They allowed one country, the United States, to sabotage the treaty, both procedurally and substantively. Whether the United Nations Framework Convention on Climate Change will survive at all is doubtful.

Well, aside from the fact that the United States is the biggest polluter in the world, and even though its empire is rapidly fading, it is still an enormously powerful nation. If a country is not its ally, it is most likely its enemy, and it can be utterly smashed, as has been demonstrated repeatedly in recent years in Yugoslavia, Iraq, Afghanistan, Somali, and (coming soon) Yemen.

In other words, what we are seeing in operation here (in the ability of the US to dictate the terms of the treaty, and even scuttle it) is the world's structure of power, obviously. The conceptual framework being used to understand and discuss this power structure, however, both inside the convention halls and outside in the streets, is badly flawed. The world is not made up of "developed" and "developing" nations. Each of the 192 nations is not separately and autonomously passing through stages to development, with some just being farther along than others. The world is made up of imperial exploiting nations and exploited or neocolonial nations. In fact, most countries of the world are not on the road to development at all. They have been and are still being systematically and deliberately underde-

Chapter 2

veloped by the core capitalist countries.

Yet these ideas were missing in Copenhagen. Capitalists were there in full force (incognito of course), but capitalism, the concept, wasn't. The negotiations were taking place, as well as the protests against them, as if capitalism didn't exist (except for a few anti-capitalist banners in the streets, and speeches by the presidents of Bolivia and Venezuela, Evo Morales and Hugo Chavez). It is not useful at all to divide the world into rich and poor countries (as the Rio treaty does). Every nation, however poor, has a rich elite, which is more or less integrated into the global capitalist system. Representatives of these elites were meeting in Copenhagen, not independent governments. Their demand that the North pay its climate debt to the South is not really about stopping global warming. It's about getting the money and technology to develop. These junior partners of empire desire to become major players. Even their insistence on democracy and transparency is colored by this desire. The first hurdle they must clear is simply to be admitted to the chambers where decisions are made.

This explains why the delegates to these conferences cannot devise effective solutions to the climate crisis. They are themselves part of the problem. Any government, after all, could, if it only wanted to, outlaw fossil fuels and enforce this law with its police and armies. There is no need to try to reduce carbon emissions through the market. They could simply be banned. This would be suicide for the capitalist class, however, of which national elites are a part, so it is never done.

Can global warming be stopped on the local level? No, it cannot. Tens of thousands of towns and cities could do everything in their power to reduce their carbon footprints and it would not make much difference as long as the great engines of capitalist industry, agriculture, transportation, government, and military are still running.

Capitalists have caused global warming.[3] It is true that

3 One of the most uncompromising statements of the link between

initially, and for a long time thereafter, capitalists didn't know that they were doing this, but they could damn well see that they were destroying the environment, and they didn't care, and still don't, any more than they cared about the millions of people they were killing, and still are. Capitalists are not going to stop global warming. They are still, and always will be, bickering and jockeying and fighting amongst themselves for position, power, markets, resources, and profits. That's what they mostly do at these conferences. (Plus, thousands of corporate lobbyists descended on Copenhagen, flushed with cash, to add to the chaotic drama).[4]

We might have survived peak oil and the gradual disappearance of cheap fossil fuel energy. (Too bad peak oil didn't happen a couple of decades earlier.) That crisis would have been spread over several decades at least. We might have had as much as 50 years to make the transition to a less energy-intensive way of life (seeing that no combination of known alternative energy sources can even begin to replace

---

capitalism and the environmental crisis is the book by Joel Kovel, *Enemy of Nature: The End of Capitalism or the End of the World?* (Zed Books, 2007, second edition, 354 pages).

4 As I understand it, originally there were only a dozen or two scientists challenging the global warming thesis, and they were obviously beholden to the fossil fuel industry. But now it seems that there are more numerous independent climatologists who challenge the prevailing view. Some of them agree that warming has been taking place but deny that this is being caused by increased levels of carbon dioxide in the atmosphere. They say it is because of normal cycles in the number of sun spots, and that the warming period we have been in will quite soon give way to cooling, probably just a normal cooling cycle, but possibly another "little ice age." Other climatologists say that the earth is not warming at all, but cooling, and they have data bases and charts to prove it. These claims are a little harder to swallow, seeing that all the glaciers are melting before our very eyes. A useful archive of papers on both sides of this debate, but with an emphasis on dissenting views, has been compiled and posted on the Global Research website in Canada, at: <http://globalresearch.ca/index.php?context=newsHighlights&newsId=24>. Let's hope that these global warming deniers are correct, and that we will get a reprieve from the imminent climate catastrophe that we are otherwise facing. However, for my part, I no longer put much stock in the arguments of the climate skeptics. It seems to me that their theories have been thoroughly refuted by the leading climate warming scientists.

Chapter 2

the energy we have been getting from fossil fuels). We would at least have had a bit more time to try once again to get capitalists out of the picture, so that humanity could work together to build a new civilization, something that is impossible to do as long as capitalists control the world. There would even have been an outside chance that it could have been a sustainable, decentralized, democratic, and just social order that we created.

But this new crisis, this imminent "tipping point" for global warming, is another beast altogether. It is happening too fast. How can we possibly dismantle in just a decade or two the vast infrastructures capitalists have built – the billions of people living in crowded metropolises, having been driven off their lands and separated from their peasant farming and now totally dependent on agribusiness for their food and on oil and gas for heat and transportation?

In retrospect, it appears that our fate was sealed when our massive communist, socialist, and anarchist movements, which mobilized tens of millions of people, failed throughout the twentieth century to defeat capitalists. Now it seems that we may not get another chance.

Can the climate justice movement stop global warming? No, it cannot. To do that it would have to be able to destroy capitalism. This objective, however, is hardly even on the agenda for most climate activists, and if it were they wouldn't have an inkling about a strategy for doing so. Hardly anyone does nowadays. If a movement can't even identify the root cause of a problem, how can it possibly solve it?

It was sweet, it's true, that climate justice activists made such an impressive showing in Copenhagen. They put 100,000 people in the streets. They came from all over the world. They organized an alternative conference, the Klima Forum. They tried to make their voices heard. But they were viciously repressed, and, in the end, actually locked out of the conference hall.

There were dozens of groups and organizations involved,

among which were: Climate Justice Action, Greenpeace International, Rising Tide International, Carbon Trade Watch, Camp for Climate Action, Friends of the Earth International, Mobilization for Climate Justice, 350.org, Rainforest Action Network, and Climate Crisis Coalition. There are hundreds of NGOs worldwide working on this issue.

Nevertheless, this movement is very short on money and power, and it is not massive (although it likes to pretend that it is). Its protests have no punch, as was noted by Naomi Klein when she said in Copenhagen: "They're laughing at us." There is not much muscle here to be coming up against a rich, deeply entrenched, historically seasoned, and powerful world ruling class. The slogans are nice: "Our Climate is Not Your Business," "Change Trade, Not the Climate," "There is No Planet B," "Bla Bla Bla, Act Now," "Nature Doesn't Compromise," and so forth. But can they ever be more than just chants? I think not.

So, what are our prospects? Realistically speaking, we are fucked. Ten, fifteen, or twenty years will go by in a flash. Business as usual will prevail. The oil, gas, and coal companies will not be reined in. The lumber companies that are cutting down the rainforests for profit will not be stopped. Corporate-controlled governments will not take action. The sheer inertia of a worldwide capitalist civilization built on cheap fossil fuel energy will keep the vast machine grinding inexorably on until the tipping point is reached, after which the irreversible warming of the earth will begin in earnest from natural causes. That will be the end of the line for us.

Further Reflections on Stopping Global Warming

In my continuing study and deliberation about global warming during the five months since the above was written, I've mostly been trying to find a little wiggle room, a

Chapter 2

way out of the dire prognosis laid out in that report on COP 15. Is our situation really as bad as I claimed?

The first thing I re-examined was the timelines on tipping points. How firm are they? Well, there are several tipping points each with an independent timeline, but which nevertheless more or less converge. Here are the major ones. (1) Death or destruction of rainforests; (2) Ocean acidification; (3) Melting of snow and ice (glaciers, ice caps on Greenland and the Antarctic, sea ice on the Arctic Ocean); (4) Ocean warming; (5) Thawing of frozen tundra across Siberia and northern Canada.

Let's take a look at these. Some scientists are now claiming that the rainforests are already at the upper limit of their tolerance for temperature increases. With further warming they might simply die, scientists say. In terms of loss of biodiversity this would be a colossal tragedy, but a tragedy also for global warming, because rainforests are a major carbon sink. They take CO_2 out of the air. If they die, they will start adding CO_2 to the atmosphere with the burning or rotting of dead trees and vegetation. Even if rainforests don't die, transnational lumber companies are cutting them down at a rapid clip, with the consent of national governments. We can't put a precise date on when they will be gone. It is not unreasonable, however, to say that if the present rate of deforestation continues, they will be gone in 20 to 30 years.[5]

The oceans are also a carbon sink, but they are becoming less so as they acidify by absorbing some of the excess CO_2 in the atmosphere. Ocean acidification is already quite alarming. It's hard to say though exactly when the oceans will stop absorbing CO_2, but 20-30 years is not an unrea-

---

[5] The top ten countries with the largest net loss of forests, 2000-2005, measured in acres of forest lost per year, are Brazil 7,667,689; Indonesia 4,623,322; Myanmar 1,151,506; Sudan 1,455,445; Zambia 1,099,614; Tanzania 1,018,070; Nigeria 1,013,127; Congo 788,263; Zimbabwe 773,436. See page 174 in Al Gore, *Our Choice*. Source: UN, FAO, *State of the World's Forests*, 2007.

sonable estimate.

The most imminent and very visible tipping point is the melting of the earth's snow and ice. This will significantly decrease the amount of sunlight being reflected back into space. Instead, the energy will stay on the earth heating up the oceans, soil, and atmosphere. Glaciers the world over are rapidly melting. The sea ice covering the Arctic Ocean is melting. The ice caps on the Antarctic and Greenland are melting. It is now believed that Greenland's ice sheet could disintegrate rapidly, in just a few decades, rather than in the century or more indicated by previous estimates.

Global warming will bring and is bringing with it drastic changes and hardships, like more severe weather, desertification, and rising sea levels. For the latter, for example, if all the snow and ice on earth melts, the sea level will rise by 250 feet. This will cause almost unimaginable suffering, destruction, and death, but is not in itself earth killing. What I want to hone in on here are the tipping points that will kill all life on earth.

It's clear what they are: warming of the oceans, and thawing of the frozen tundra stretching across Siberia and northern Canada. Why? Because this warming will release billions of tons of methane gas trapped in the northern permafrost and in frozen nodules in the oceans (methane hydrates). (And methane is a more powerful greenhouse gas than carbon dioxide.) Once this process is fully underway it becomes self-perpetuating and is irreversible. There are no natural processes that could remove the gas from the atmosphere fast enough. The atmosphere will become poisonous. The earth will get very hot. All life will die. The earth will become like Venus.[6]

This is what we must fear. If carbon dioxide emissions are not stopped, the earth will continue to heat up. Carbon dioxide in the atmosphere is continuing to increase by 2 ppm (parts per million) per year. Thus in 20 years

---

[6] See Chapter 10, "The Venus Syndrome," in James Hansen, *Storms of My Grandchildren*.

Chapter 2

another 40 ppm will be added to the existing 385 ppm, which is already 35 ppm over the 350 ppm which is considered the maximum permissible for a stable climate. (The pre-industrial level was 280 ppm in 1750.) 425 ppm CO2 might be enough to raise the earth's temperature another two degrees. So, these last two tipping points could well be passed in twenty years, thirty at the most.[7] These dates are not absolutely firm, but seeing that all life on earth is at stake, we dare not gamble that we have more time. The permafrost has already started to thaw, releasing gas, and methane has already been observed bubbling up in the Arctic Ocean and elsewhere. Stopping this is our most urgent task.

Before returning to the question of whether or how global warming can be stopped, let me set the scene a little more clearly with some pertinent facts. As most everyone now knows, carbon dioxide is the most important greenhouse gas, comprising 76.7% of the total. Of this, 56.6% comes from burning fossil fuels; another 17.3% comes from deforestation and rotting vegetation; and 2.8% from other sources. Other major greenhouse gases are methane at 14.3%, and nitrous oxide at 7.9%.[8]

So, this is why the focus has been on reducing CO2. Most of the CO2 from burning fossil fuels comes from burning coal to generate electricity. Forty-one percent of electricity worldwide is generated from burning coal (gas 20%, hydro 16%, nuclear 15%, oil 6%, renewable 2%).[9] Being new to the issue I found this surprising. I had assumed that most emissions came from burning oil (gasoline, diesel, kero-

---

[7] For the December essay I had picked up the year 2020 from various reports and target dates circulating at Copenhagen. Upon further study, however, I think that ten years is too early to expect tipping points to be passed. We have a little more time than that, but not much, 20-30 years.

[8] From a diagram on page 8, Anna Lappe, *Diet for a Hot Planet*. Source: International Panel on Climate Change, 4th Assessment, "Synthesis Report."

[9] Source: World Coal Institute. "Total World Electricity Generation by Fuel (2006)." On the web at: <http://www.worldcoal.org/coal/uses-of-coal/coal-electricity/>

sene) in cars, trucks, and planes. Actually, transportation accounts for about half as many emissions as coal-fired power plants.

The breakdown of carbon dioxide emissions by sector of the economy is as follows, in descending order of size: energy supply 25.9%, industry 19.4%, forestry 17.4%, agriculture 13.5%, transportation 13.1%, residential and commercial buildings 7.9%, and waste and wastewater 2.8%.[10] So all the stress being put on greening residential and commercial buildings while ignoring electricity generation, industry, and agriculture is seriously misguided.

Where, geographically, do CO2 emissions come from? Again, there is a surprise, since everyone says that the United States is the worst polluter. This is not true if Europe is taken as a whole (and after all they've been toting their European Union for some time now), and if we include Russia as part of Europe as it rightfully should be. Thus in 2008 China produced 22.1% of CO2 emissions, with Europe at 20.7%, the United States at 17.9%, and the rest of the world at 39.3% (India 3.5%, Japan 4.1%). Historically (1751-2008), Europe is seen to be an even worse polluter with 37.9% of cumulative emissions to the US's 27.2%, and China's 9.1%.[11]

These facts suggest a point of attack, and James Hansen has been focusing on it for some time: coal.[12] If the world would stop burning coal to generate electricity this alone would significantly reduce carbon emissions, perhaps enough so to slow global warming a bit to give us more time to get off fossil fuels altogether. We can narrow it down even further. If only the United States (with 614 coal-fired power plants, out of 2300 worldwide) and China (with 620

---

[10] From a diagram on page 10, Anna Lappe, *Diet for a Hot Planet*. Source: International Panel on Climate Change, 4th Assessment Report, "Synthesis Report."

[11] From two diagrams on page 189, James Hansen, *Storms of My Grandchildren*.

[12] See, for example, James Hansen, "Coal-fired power stations are death factories. Close them." *The Observer*, Sunday, February 15, 2009.

coal-fired power plants, with about 500 more due to come on-line in the near future) would stop burning coal this would be a big step toward reducing CO2 emissions. But how likely is it that these two nations, each with a rapacious and savage capitalist ruling class, can be pressured to do so? Not very damn likely, I'd say.

No, global warming is a global problem and requires a global solution. Even if the US, Europe, and China, which together produce 60% of the world's total, all reduced their CO2 emissions to zero, that would still leave the 40% being produced by the rest of the world. That 40% might be enough to push us over the tipping points.

It seems unlikely also that coal could be separated out like this from the rest of the problem. If a global campaign could be organized and implemented to phase out coal why not also work to get off fossil fuels in general at the same time. That would make more sense. But just to replace all coal-fired power plants in the world would in itself take a stupendous amount of capital, involvement of all major governments, and agreement by a sizable chunk of the corporate and financial elite. There would have to be a worldwide coordinated effort to rapidly exploit, on a massive scale, all alternative sources of energy for the generation of electricity – wind, solar, geothermal, tides, heat pumps – and do this without building more dams or nuclear power plants. Such an international crash program does not seem in the cards at all. In fact, the opposite is happening. At least three dozen countries are in the process of building more coal-fired power plants.

The task of getting off all fossil fuels is even more daunting. It would require, in addition to clean electricity, massive energy conservation programs, abandonment of industrial agriculture in favor of sustainable organic farming, retro-fitting the world's cars and trucks for hydrogen or electricity and a drastic reduction in their number, massive investment in high speed electric trains and other public transportation, severe curtailment of flying, resettlement of the countryside, stopping the destruction of forests, drastic reduction of energy use almost across the board, putting an end to waste and shoddy products, abandonment of unnecessary or frivolous industry, dismantling the world's military machines (which are among the greatest consumers of oil, especially the Pentagon), abolition of stock markets, defeat of the mammoth oil companies, and so forth.

Just to list these minimum required changes exposes how utterly incompatible they are with capitalism, for those who are even aware of capitalism, that is, and understand how it works. Capitalists have caused these human-made material realities we are living with – the 438 nuclear power plants with 61 more under construction (as of 2010), the roughly 800 million passenger cars and light trucks on the road (in 2007), the megacities (20 of them with a population of over 10 million each, another 26 with a population of over 5 million each), the fleets of jet planes, oil tankers, agribusiness, skyscrapers, industry, tourism, the huge government bureaucracies, massive dams, and so forth. Are capitalists likely to do an about face now and start to dismantle all this? No they're not. They couldn't, actually (and remain capitalists, that is), because there is no profit to be made from dismantling all this infrastructure.

It's true that a small minority of capitalists are trying to make profit off global warming. They are building vast wind and solar installations, inventing hydrogen powered cars, converting millions of acres of farm land to the production of biomass, trying to create a market for carbon trading, and starting to build vast new power grids. When corporations and governments do get involved in trying to stop global warming, this is the direction they go in. They try to solve the crisis within the framework of capitalism. Even many of the most outspoken climate activists do this; that is, they are not anti-capitalist – James Hansen, George Monbiot, Bill McKibben, Al Gore, or Ross Gelbspan. Those few climate theorists who are anti-capitalist,

Chapter 2

mostly from a Marxist perspective, nevertheless think that the crisis can be solved with the aid of governments – Joel Kovel, John Bellamy Foster, Charles Derber. That is, they are anti-capitalist, but not anti-state. This is just to say that an anarchist perspective on the crisis is hardly in the discussion at all (but see Recommended Essays below).

At least one head of state, Evo Morales, president of Bolivia, has clearly identified capitalism as the enemy, when he said "Either capitalism dies or Mother Earth dies." But as the head of a government he naturally doesn't think of attacking the state too, or representative government *per se*. According to one participant in April's climate justice conference in Tiquipaya, Bolivia, many of those attending (roughly 30,000 from 140 countries, with 40 governmental delegations) were anti-capitalists, but few were anti-state. Besides, Evo Morales is merely president of one of the poorest nations on earth. How much power does he have? Where are the voices of the great European labor unions, the big UN agencies like the World Health Organization or the Food and Agriculture Organization, the global NGOs, the leaders of the world's Social Democratic parties?

At this point a conceptual clarification is necessary in order to grasp the scope of the problem and to begin to perceive the necessary solution. Capitalism is the name for an entire social order. It is not just an "economy." Thus, the international nation-state system is an integral part of capitalism, and has been from the very beginning. Capitalists took over the pre-existing state forms and turned them to their own ends, integrating them into their project of accumulating capital. The ability to make profit from privately owned productive properties would be impossible without the legal framework provided by governments, backed by police and military violence. Businesses and governments are in bed together, and have been for the past five hundred years (profit takers + politicians = capitalism). Yet even when a few climate justice activists do admit that capitalism has to be destroyed in order to stop global warming, they fail to note that states do too. Except for anarchists.

Global warming, after all, is merely the end result of centuries of environmental ravaging by capitalists. They have been destroying the environment from their earliest days as the world's most powerful ruling class. Earlier civilizations did too, but not on such a scale, nor with such relentlessness, nor with a logic internal to their social system, nor with powerful industrial technology, nor were they global civilizations. Capitalists can't make profit without externalizing the environmental costs. It is foolish therefore to think that global warming can be stopped within a capitalist framework.

Once the true root cause of the climate crisis has been identified – the entire global social order known as capitalism – it is not difficult to map out the long-term solution. An entirely new civilization must be built. This will be a decentralized world without borders, without states, with production for use not profit, based on cooperation and mutual aid, without wage-slavery, money, markets, or hierarchy, a self-governing global social order based on direct democracy. There is a very rich tradition of social philosophy – namely, anarchism (especially anarcho-communism) – which has been explicitly agitating for such a social arrangement for nearly two hundred years (but of course actual anarchist practices stretch back for millennia, and are worldwide). There is no space here to describe in detail what such a civilization might look like or how it might be achieved. I must be content to refer the reader to the extensive anarchist literature. If anyone needs a leg up, they could consult my work, *Anarchy. An Introductory Bibliography in English*.

So this is the extraordinary task we face ("we," meaning we the world's ordinary people, all people, not just indigenous people). We must take decision making away from the ruling class and restore it to our households, workplaces, and communities. We must decommodify everything and reassemble ourselves socially. An entire social order, a global civilization, organized on the basis of profit-mongering, must be defeated in the next twenty to thirty years or else we all die, not just human beings, but every living creature on earth. We no longer have the option of going back to barbarism and starting over ("socialism or barbarism"). That option has been eliminated by global warming. Our only option now is Anarchy or Death. This is a powerful incentive. This will be our last (and perhaps best) chance to break the stranglehold capitalists have had on us for five hundred years, to create a new society, and to save ourselves and life on earth.

Can this be done? Quite frankly, I don't see how. But we must try. It will require an unprecedented, massive, global anti-capitalist (including an anti-statist) movement. There are tentative signs that such a movement is emerging and gathering steam, as was perhaps indicated a bit by the climate conference in Bolivia last April. We all must do everything in our power to strengthen and build this movement. It is our only hope.

Recommended Essays

Anonymous, *Introduction to the Apocalypse*. 2009, 68 pages. On the web in the *Zine Library*, at: <http://zinelibrary.info/introduction-apocalypse-0>.
Also in the *Anarchist Library* at: <http:/theanarchistlibrary.org/HTML/Anonymous__Introduction_to_the_Apocalypse.html>.
COP15 Zine Crew, *Dealing with Distractions: Confronting Green Capitalism in Copenhagen and Beyond* (various authors), 2009, 32 pages, posted on *Anarchist Library*, <http://theanarchistlibrary.org/HTML/Various_Authors__Dealing_with_Distractions__Confronting_Green_Capitalism_in_Copenhagen_and_Beyond.html>.
DeAngelis, Massimo, "Mother Earth, states and

commons: reflections on "el cumbri"," posted on *The Commoner*, May 21, 2010, at: <http://www.commoner.org.uk:80/blog/?p=243>.

Flood, Andrew, "Transport, Volcano's, CO2, and the Planned Economy," April 20, 2010, posted on *Anarchist Writers* at: <http://anarchism.pageabode.com/andrewnflood/transport-volcanos-economy-co2>.

Gelderloos, Peter, "Capitalist Solutions for Global Warming: More Wood for the Fire," posted on *Counterpunch*, February 1, 2010, at: <http://www.counterpunch.org/gelderloos02012010.html>.

Gelderloos, Peter, "Before the Big Change," 2009, posted on *Anarchist Library*, at: <http://theanarchistlibrary.org/HTML/Peter_Gelderloos__Before_the_Big_Change.html>

Simons, Tim, and Ali Tonak, "The Dead End of Climate Justice: How NGO Bureaucrats and Greenwashed Corporations are Turning Nature into Investment Capital," posted on *Counterpunch*, Weekend Edition, January 8-10, 2010, at: <http://www.counterpunch.org/simons01082010.html>.

A Short Bibliography

Christianson, Gale E., *Greenhouse: The 200-Year Story of Global Warming*. New York: Walker, 1999, 305 pages.

Derber, Charles, *Greed to Green: Solving Climate Change and Remaking the Economy*. Boulder, Colorado: Paradigm Publishers, 2010, 268 pages.

Dimento, Joseph F. C., and Pamela Doughman, editors, *Climate Change: What It Means for Us, Our Children, and Our Grandchildren.* Cambridge, Massachusetts: MIT Press, 2007, 217 pages.

Foster, John Bellamy, *The Ecological Revolution: Making Peace with the Planet.* New York: Monthly Review Press, 2009, 328 pages.

Gelbspan, Ross, *Boiling Point: How Politicians, Big Oil and Coal, Journalists, and Activists are Fueling the Climate Crisis – and What We Can Do to Avert Disaster.* New York: Basic Books, 2004, 254 pages.

Gelbspan, Ross, *The Heat Is On: The High Stakes Battle Over Earth's Threatened Climate.* New York: Addison-Wesley, 1997, 287 pages.

Gore, Al, *Our Choice: A Plan to Solve the Climate Crisis.* Emmaus, Pennsylvania: Rodale, 2009, 416 pages.

Hansen, James, *Storms of My Grandchildren: The Truth about the Coming Climate Catastrophe and Our Last Chance to Save Humanity.* New York: Bloomsbury, 2009, 304 pages.

Kovel, Joel, *The Enemy of Nature: The End of Capitalism or the End of the World?* London: Zed Books, 2002, 273 pages.

Lappe, Anna, *Diet for a Hot Plant: The Climate Crisis at the End of Your Fork and What You Can Do About It.* New York: Bloomsbury, 2010, 313 pages.

McKibben, Bill, *Eaarth: Making a Life on a Tough New Planet.* New York: Henry Holt, 2010, 253 pages.

McKibben, Bill, *Fight Global Warming Now: The Handbook for Taking Action in Your Community.* New York: Henry Holt, 2007, 202 pages.

Monbiot, George, *Heat: How to Stop the Planet from Burning.* Cambridge, Massachusetts: South End Press, 2007, 277 pages.

Motavalli, Jim, editor, *Feeling the Heat: Dispatches from*

the Frontlines of Climate Change. New York: Routledge, 2004, 194 pages.

Shiva, Vandana, *Soil Not Oil: Environmental Justice in an Age of Climate Crisis.* Cambridge, Massachusetts: South End Press, 2008, 145 pages.

Weart, Spencer R., *The Discovery of Global Warming.* Cambridge, Massachusetts: Harvard University Press, 2003, 228 pages.

3

Is Greed All That is Wrong with Capitalism?

August, 1999

*I**s greed all that's wrong with capitalism?* No. It is not enough to attack capitalists for being greedy, although this is a common tactic. I hope to explain why in this short essay.

Consider a small business family who work longer hours than do their employees, who live frugally, keeping just enough of the income from the business to support their modest lifestyle, paying the rest out in wages to their employees. If greed were all that is wrong with capitalism then these capitalists would be considered exemplary and above criticism, because in no way are they greedy. But they are still in charge! As bosses or managers. And this is the crux of the matter. They still own the properties, the means of production. Their employees don't. They are buyers of waged-labor; their employees are sellers of waged-labor. Thus their employees are slaves, wage-slaves. They are not. There is an inequality here, of power, status, class, and wealth, which is built into the system, and based on the private ownership of properties. So even if the annual financial return from the business is roughly the same for employers and employees, it is still an unjust social arrangement and must be morally condemned.

This hypothetical case has not been all that common in history, but then neither has it been exactly rare. There have been some proprietors like this. It's true of course that most proprietors have tried to get richer, but it's also true that many have failed to do so. There have always been millions of small business families and self-employed tradesmen who were barely surviving, and cannot be said to have had a significantly higher standard of living than many wage-earners.

Although there were a few large joint stock companies even in the early days of capitalism (the East India Company was established in Britain in 1600), giant corporations did not become prominent until late in the 19th century, and then mostly in heavy industry. Throughout most of the five-century history of capitalism small proprietors have been the mainstay of the system (although not the greatest profit takers; those have been the large monopolies which have always existed). It is only now, at the end of the twentieth century, with the phenomenal concentration of capital that has taken place in the past half century in all sectors, including farming, banking, retail, trade, services, publishing, medicine, law, transport, media, and so on, that the petty bourgeoisie is really disappearing from the scene, especially in the more thoroughly capitalist countries.

I have recalled this brief history as a prelude to getting at the question of greed. I believe that for the small proprietor the driving motive has not been greed, but simply survival. Business has been a way of making a living, getting along, and providing for oneself and one's family. For parents, the protective instinct, the desire to provide for the children and ensure their survival, safety, and well-being, is surely much stronger than mere greed. It is a desire for security that undergirds capitalism, as much as anything. People like to feel safe and unthreatened and to have the resources to meet life's emergencies – a sick child, a damaging accident, a dying mate, economic depressions, floods and droughts, earthquakes and tornadoes. At what point can it be said that anyone has enough to be really secure? This is a fuzzy line. It takes quite a lot of money before anyone feels that they never have to worry again. And even after the immediate family is provided for, there are always relatives, and grandchildren, and numerous projects that need to be done. Also, there is always the chance, given the incredible turmoil and chaos that characterize capitalism as a system, that a family might lose everything, in a crash, bankruptcy, or revolution. So when is anyone ever going to feel that they have too much?

Take a small town capitalist family whose business is successful, and who are thus able to send their children to a good college, build a big new home in a nice part of town, drive a new car, and take vacations to the West Indies. Is this all based on greed? No, it is just a normal desire to live well and be happy, which everyone has. Practically everyone, except for ascetics, would like to be free from poverty and toil, and to enjoy the good things of life.

So their motivation is not the problem. The problem is that under capitalism their well-being is gained by the impoverishment of others. And this is for structural reasons, not motivational ones. That is, it is because the world has become divided into people who buy labor power and people who sell labor power. There are only these two choices: you are either in business for yourself or you are a hired hand. But our small town capitalist family can't blame themselves for this. They did not make things this way. They were born into an already existing social order. It's all they know. They may consider it unfortunate that some people are poor, but they do not see it as any fault of theirs. On the contrary, they probably see it as the fault of the poor themselves, because they have not succeeded, whereas they themselves (our entrepreneurs) have. They most likely even feel that they deserve what they have, because they have worked hard for it (and most small pro-

Chapter 3

prietors do work hard).

Let's go back a ways, to the beginnings of capitalism, and take a look at the situation then. It used to be thought that capitalism was established by the bourgeoisie overthrowing the landed aristocracy, so that one class replaced another, as rulers, over a period of time. Now however we know that this is only partially true. There was considerable carry over among ruling class families from feudalism to capitalism. That is, many aristocrats managed to turn themselves into capitalists, and thus to stay in the ruling class. This was done mostly through capitalist agriculture, but also by members of the landed aristocracy going into trade, and becoming merchants themselves. As feudalism was collapsing, a new way of extracting the surplus wealth from the direct producers had to be found. The invention of capitalism was the answer to this need. The old rulers were active in this process as well as the new burgers. To speak of this historical process as being motivated by greed is to considerably oversimplify. The burgers of course were mostly small scale entrepreneurs trying to make a living, but doing it in a new way (by living off profit). As for the aristocrats, they were rulers seeking to preserve themselves and their families and stay in power, and not be done in, abolished, or overthrown. This involved the desire for power too, as well as money, the desire to survive, the desire to maintain a traditional way of life, the desire to maintain control, in order to go on living well, and so forth. What would happen to them if the existing order were changed or destroyed? Would heads roll? Would they lose everything? It is fear, more than greed, that drives them. They are afraid for their lives. If the existing social order collapses, they may end up not only poor, but dead.

Similarly with the creation of the class of landless wage-earners. The traditional image is that of landowners forcing peasants off the commons and off their peasant holdings, so that this land could be enclosed by the lords in order to grow sheep for wool for sale to the textile indus-

Is Greed All That is Wrong with Capitalism?

try. Recent research has established however that the proletariat was created in part from below. A peasant family would somehow acquire an extra field or two, and would eventually need help working this extra land, so they would hire help. And so emerged a class of more well-to-do peasants and a larger class of peasants who had less land than before and who hired out as wage-earners to supplement their incomes. These wealthier peasant families were in the same situation as the small business family discussed above. They were simply trying to live a little better and to have a little more security.

I have no problem with anyone's wanting to be rich. I would like to be rich myself. I want more, of everything. I want to be able to enjoy the good things of life. I think everyone should be rich. And there's the rub. Under capitalism, just as under all previous social orders based on hierarchy and class, everyone does not get rich. A few get rich, while most remain poor. In fact, the few are rich precisely because the many are poor, because the wealth of the few is stolen wealth, taken from the labors of the many. If we were all getting rich together, and if this were accomplished without destroying the earth, it would be another thing entirely. It would be paradise on earth.

One problem with the focus on greed as the main problem of capitalism is that it contributes to an impulse toward austerity. It leads some people to argue that we should give up what we have and live frugally, and to cut back and consume less. This tendency was quite pronounced in the New Left of the sixties in the United States. It's true that this impulse was also based on the belief that the high standard of living in the United States was made possible only by ripping off the rest of the world, and also on the belief that such a high standard of living could not be maintained, certainly not for the whole world, without destroying the earth. But these two beliefs need not have led anyone to embrace austerity. They might have led instead to struggles to equalize the wealth, so that everyone could be better

Chapter 3

off, and to the search for ways of creating wealth which do not destroy the earth.

But this has not happened, at least not on a very big scale. Instead, we have 'voluntary poverty' – large numbers of radicals voluntarily embracing a reduced life – restricted travel, inadequate shelter, fewer clothes, fewer tools, less entertainment, fewer vacations, no money to undertake projects, less education, less security against accidents and sickness, a hand to mouth existence, and so forth. (I am not talking of course about radicals who live frugally in order to have time and resources for the struggle.)

This has been a big mistake, I think, and is certainly not the way to destroy capitalism. You cannot convince people to oppose capitalism by asking them to give up what they already have. You have to convince them that they could be even richer, and have a higher standard of living, and a better quality of life, under another social arrangement, and that this could be true for everyone, and be done without destroying the earth. The desire to be secure and well off is a very powerful human motivation that should not be confused with greed.

Another problem with the idea of greed as a critique of capitalism is that it shifts the focus to individuals and away from relations between individuals, that is, away from the structure of the system (patterned relationships among people). Greed is a characteristic of an individual. It is a personality trait, a character flaw, a moral failing. The remedy for greed is to get individuals to be better, to improve themselves spiritually. This leads to preaching, to moralizing, to the effort to change individuals into less greedy people. It is a religious task, a job for priests and evangelists. It lacks a social dimension. This sermonizing completely bypasses, therefore, or even derails, the struggle between classes over power and the ownership and distribution of wealth.

Far more powerful and accurate, than the notion of

greed, is the idea of exploitation. This was the original moral condemnation of capitalism that emerged in the early nineteenth century. This is a social idea; exploitation takes at least two persons. It characterizes a relationship. It is not a name for an individual moral failure. Capitalism is condemned because it is based on the exploitation of one class by another, so that the exploiting class can enrich itself, or simply remain in power. Even earlier, say in the English revolution of the seventeenth century, the class system of rich and poor, of lords and peasants, was also condemned in moral terms, for being unjust. The radical critique of capitalism (and before that, peasant critiques of feudalism) has always been based on a ethical condemnation of the system, and not just the moral failings of individuals within the ruling class. It is not just that someone is getting rich, it is their getting rich at the expense of others that is the problem.

By the mid-nineteenth century, capitalism had come to be understood as a system of theft. (Marx was largely responsible for this, by proving that profit came from unpaid wages rather than from the sale of the product.) Stealing of course is a lot bigger crime than mere greed. (Is greed a crime at all, or only a sin?) If this theft is backed up with murder, not to mention all kinds of lesser abuses, then the moral condemnation of capitalism begins to take on some bite. There are plenty of greedy people who are nevertheless unwilling to resort to theft and murder to satisfy their cravings. It is the willingness of someone to back up their greed with stealing (and worse) that turns them into criminals, not just their desire to get rich. Since capitalism is inherently a system of theft, and since capitalists, as a class, do regularly and systematically resort to lying, brutality, torture, oppression, murder, and war to defend their scam, capitalists are not merely greedy, they are outright criminals. It is by portraying and exposing capitalists as the criminals they are that we can begin to break through their ideological defenses and destroy their credibility.

It is true however that this ethical aspect of the radical rejection of capitalism was muted, or sometimes lost all together, during the many decades when "scientific marxism" held sway over anti-capitalist movements. During these decades many activists believed that the collapse of capitalism was inevitable, because of the laws of history and the internal dynamics of the system itself. These beliefs tended to mute or negate the moral dimension of their struggles, and caused them to lose sight of the fact that they were fighting against injustice. Beginning with the New Left in the sixties an effort has been made by many radicals to recover the moral high ground (which has largely been captured by the far right) and to reinstate the ethical dimension of anti-capitalist struggles.

The stress on greed is perhaps part of this. Greed is mentioned as a counter to the idea of 'economic determinism' so characteristic of vulgar, mechanical Marxism. This is a way of saying that it is not the laws of history that are askew, but the concrete moral failings of real people. It is a way of rejecting the idea that economics determines everything, and of reinstating a role for human agency. Unfortunately, as I have been explaining, 'greed' is not exactly the right tool for the job. Other weapons in the radical arsenal are more powerful, like 'exploitation', or even 'alienation' (another concept that stresses the social aspects of a relationship – the alienation of workers, by property owners, from the products of their labor, and from the process of labor itself, so that they become mere tools in someone else's hands). 'Criminality' is an even more powerful accusation. In most countries there are laws against things that capitalists do regularly. Rather than criticizing capitalists for being greedy, we should be arresting them for being criminals.

The stress on greed as the main problem of capitalism leads to other misguided campaigns, like the 'living wage campaign' or the demand for 'socially responsible corporations'. The living wage campaign is not a fight against capitalism, but only against low wages. Wages have once again dropped so low for millions of workers, even in the rich countries, that they won't support life. Corporations, it is said, are taking too much in profit; they are being greedy; they should keep less for themselves, their stockholders, and their executives, and pay higher wages to their employees instead. Thus rather than trying to abolish a system wherein some live off wages while others live off profits, these activists are limiting their demands to merely getting a 'living wage'. It reminds me a little of that older, similarly absurd slogan, 'a fair day's pay for a fair day's work.' Under capitalism there is no such thing as a fair day's pay. It is structurally impossible. The system is inherently unfair, being based on the siphoning off, through force, of part of the wealth created by the direct producers.

The recent clamor, by many progressives, for 'socially responsible corporations' is another misguided campaign, and also stems in part from the idea of greed. It is assumed that corporations could, if only they weren't so greedy, be more generous and responsible. This assumption, however, misjudges the nature of the beast. Corporations, by their very nature, are inherently irresponsible. They could not survive, for example, if they had to absorb all the external costs of their operations. They could not possibly make a profit. Being able to externalize (fob off onto the public) many of the costs of production is almost a definition of capitalism, as a system of competing, profit-based, corporations, supported by nation-states. Nor could they survive very long if they raised wages very much, or spent money on safety, because other corporations wouldn't and would therefore drive them out of business. We need to keep this struggle among capitalists in mind when looking at sweatshops, unsafe mines, and toxic workplaces, and not limit our criticisms to the cruelty and greed of capitalists, but direct it to the system itself (although obviously such capitalists have to be able to at least stomach what they are doing, which is already a strong indictment of their characters).

On the other hand, when we do see the occasional corporation that 'does right by its employees', as they like to claim, with 'decent' wages, pension plans, profit-sharing, sick leave, good vacations, maternity leave, grievance procedures, eight hour days, and so forth, we have to remember that this is still based on wage-slavery, on the expropriation of wealth from the direct producers, and is thus an unjust set up. Furthermore, such beneficial policies came into being originally in the context of a strong labor movement, which raised the standards for all workers, even those in nonunion workplaces. Now that unions are practically gone in the United States, benefits like these have been disappearing rapidly. It's doubtful that such 'liberal' corporations will last much longer in the current period of corporate ascendency. Most Americans are already working longer hours, at a faster pace, for less pay, than they were thirty years ago. In short, the campaign for 'socially responsible corporations' is ridiculous, totally reformist, and completely unable to solve the social and ecological crises that are overwhelming humanity under late twentieth century capitalism.

Many corporations do try of course to portray themselves as socially responsible, mainly by giving away money to good causes, like symphony orchestras, the arts, scientific research, education, and the like, such moneys often taking the place of public funding for these activities (funding which has been gutted from government budgets by corporate-bought legislators). I always thought that if a company had so much extra money that it could give it away, it should either raise the wages of its employees or lower the prices of its products. It has no business getting into philanthropy. Quite obviously though, corporations use this largess as a public relations ploy; the expenditure can be considered part of their advertising budget; it is designed to improve their corporate images. If the public becomes concerned about the environment, before long corporations will start giving themselves a green wash. Just as the Fords, Mellons, and Rockefellers, in earlier times, set up philanthropic foundations, to give away millions for good causes (but good causes, by the way, which never challenged the system itself), to try to diminish somewhat the public's anger at their plunder, so do our contemporary super corporations constantly try to enhance their images by giving to worthy causes. Corporate giving of course doesn't begin to replace the deleted public funding. Also, much contemporary corporate philanthropy is not done through semi-independent foundations, but directly by the corporations themselves; it is therefore even more blatantly sheer self-aggrandizement.

Sometimes the criticism is broadened a bit, beyond simple greed, to the 'institutionalization of greed'. This idea is somewhat more useful, but not by much. Every class society since the dawn of history could be described as the 'institutionalization of greed', but this would not be saying very much about them. It would not tell us what is distinctive about these societies and in most cases would even distort their functioning. Most importantly, it would not explain the mechanisms through which the surplus wealth was expropriated from one class by another.

Capitalism might be defined as the 'institutionalization of the profit-motive', but the profit-motive is not at all the same as greed. Anti-capitalist radicals too often focus almost exclusively on the struggle between capital and labor, to the neglect of the very serious struggles among capitalists themselves. These latter struggles account for a lot of what happens under capitalism. If a capitalist enterprise doesn't make a profit, it disappears, vanishes, goes out of existence. It either goes bankrupt or else is gobbled up by a larger, more profitable company. From the point of view of the corporation, the need to turn a profit, and as big a profit as possible, is absolute. It is the first requirement for survival. Turning a profit means expanding, finding new markets, making new products. This is necessary because of the pressures of other corporations, all of which are trying to do the same thing.

In the nineteen nineties we are living through one of the most intense periods of the concentration of capital (mergers, or the big fish gobbling up the little fish) in the history of capitalism. These mergers have been triggered by pressures on the rate of profit throughout the world. This tendency to merge is inherent to the system, stemming from the competition among firms to stay profitable (and therefore to stay in existence), and, needless to say, from pressures from below, from the working class, which also puts a squeeze on profits. So corporations get bigger and bigger. The idea that we can go backwards, to a capitalism made up of millions of small scale proprietors, is completely unrealistic. Yet this assumption underlies much of populist protest and agitation in the United States. These populists do not direct their anger against capitalism itself, but only against giant corporations.

This analysis shows that even for the big boys, operating in a world market composed of viciously competing, profit-based corporations, survival is the driving force, not greed. The idea that any of these firms could, if they were only so inclined (that is, if only they were run by nicer people), start behaving in more generous and responsible ways, is a total illusion. Sometimes corporations can be forced to behave responsibly by government regulation of a whole industry, which eliminates the competitive advantage for any individual firm which behaves irresponsibly. But we are now in the midst of a great period of deregulation. Neo-liberals have launched a sustained assault on government regulation of business. Governments are thus losing the power to reign in individual corporations or industries, in order to protect capitalism as a whole. That is, they are losing the ability to act in the interests of capitalists as a class (unless the interests of the class truly lies in neo-liberalism, weakened national governments, and the new world order; but I doubt that they are). Given this situation, populists who are clamoring for 'socially responsible corporations' are acting rather naively, perhaps even irresponsibly.

Another notion sometimes used to diagnose our current situation is the 'culture of materialism', which is somewhat connected to the idea of greed, which is why I'm mentioning it. It is thought that our problems stem from ourselves. We are too materialistic. We are too addicted to 'things'. The solution to the dire straits the world is in, according to this view, is for us to slough off this materialism, reform ourselves, stop wanting everything, and learn to live more simply. I have problems with this idea.

For one thing, I believe that most human communities throughout history have been materialistic. They have had to be in order to survive. They have had to provide a certain quantity of essential material things for themselves in order to live – food, shelter, clothing, tools, transportation, weapons. I doubt though that persons who complain about the culture of materialism are talking about these bare necessities. They are talking about things you don't need. But this is a little tricky. Needs are socially defined. An item which is considered unnecessary in one culture, may be considered quite essential by the average person in another culture. Beyond bare necessities of nourishment and shelter from cold, human needs are almost completely culturally defined, and vary considerably, historically and across cultures. And why shouldn't they? Why shouldn't different peoples have different tastes and different ways of satisfying their needs? And why shouldn't our needs expand as we become richer? Why shouldn't we try to enrich our lives as much as we can?

For another thing, I believe that the 'culture of materialism', as the idea is being used currently, is quite obviously a product of capitalism itself. Under the incessant drive to sell, sell, sell, corporations strive mightily to create needs, and bring into being a demand for their products and services. Advertising is an enormous industry, incessantly pressuring us to buy. Many other social pressures also get us to buy commodities. The average person is a victim of this culture of materialism, not its cause. This might be called a false materialism, or a materialism that has run amok. We probably shouldn't even call this materialism, however, but 'commodification,' 'commercialism,' or 'consumerism.' I shop, you shop, we shop, they profit. It is the culture of capitalism, which has promoted a whole set of needs, a whole schedule of irrational priorities, that might even be regarded as nonmaterial, since they lead to death, rather than sustain life. Some capitalists value profit more than life itself.

Many of the needs we have might not be considered necessary in another society, but are essential in this one. We are locked into many of these needs. Most of us need a car, for example, to commute to work and drive to a supermarket miles away (in the absence of work closer to home, public transportation, or corner grocery stores). We need our own house or an apartment, in the absence of communal or cooperative housing. We need a refrigerator, since much of the available food needs to be kept cold. We need machines to wash our clothes, and either have to buy these machines or rent them. We need a stove to cook our food on. And so forth. Capitalism has rebuilt (in a very haphazard and irrational way) almost the entire human material world, and in the process has locked us into a multitude of needs which cannot be abolished just by wishing. We will have to change practically the entire social world and then rebuild the physical plant within which we live in order to eliminate many of these needs.

So what is urgently needed is for us to redefine what it means to live really well and enjoy a high quality life. But this cannot be done abstractly. It must be done as part of the struggle to oppose the destructive definitions of wealth and well-being that have been thrown up by the capitalist imperative to maximize profit for the owners. The material look of a truly free society, one created to facilitate the highest possible development of every individual, would be strikingly different than the one we now live in.

There is a slightly different angle on this to consider. Rather than criticize ourselves for being materialistic, we might try criticizing capitalists for preventing us from meeting our material needs. The truth is, that despite all the glittering commodities, capitalism doesn't deliver the material goods. We are left wanting. We have umpteen urgent material needs that are not being met – the simple need for food, clothing, and shelter (for billions of people), the need for nutritious food (for most of us in the rich countries), the need for clean air, the need for time to play, sleep, love, dance, sing, the need for clean water (an increasingly rare item), the need for an unpolluted environment, the need for meaningful work, the need for neighbors, the need for safe and nontoxic workplaces, the need for parks, the need for swimming pools and bicycle paths, the need for resources to travel. The list of our unmet material needs is long.

A slight variation on the 'culture of materialism' theme is the 'culture of greed'. There can be no doubt that capitalism has thrown up a 'culture of greed', but this does not mean that it is the motor which runs the system. The culture of greed is more the outcome of the normal operation of the profit-motive, rather than its cause, just as are fanatic individualism, competitiveness, the fetishism of privacy, people without memories, materialism, and all the other dimensions of the culture of capitalism. Capitalists have not only erected the social institutions they need, but have brought into being an entire cultural apparatus to support their practices, and even worse, have shaped our very personalities and character structures to fit the prerequisites of a profit driven system. The disappearance of all other values, leaving just commercial ones, is thus a result not a cause. But this result is definitely there – masses of indi-

Chapter 3

viduals looking out only for themselves, trying to get as much as they can, any way that they can, with very narrow definitions of the quality of life, of material enrichment, and of well-being. But individualism, competitiveness, and greed cannot simply be exorcised from our personalities, directly, on a person to person basis, through exhortation, but can be eliminated, in the long run, and on a massive scale, only by destroying social arrangements founded on the profit-motive, wage-slavery, and private property. Of course first there have to be people who want to do this.

Let's consider now a group of corporations engaged in more than murder. The one hundred or so giant corporations that produce the bulk of the world's coal, oil, and natural gas, the burning of which is warming the earth, are not just thieves and murderers, but are rapidly becoming guilty of genocide, ecocide, and possibly even planetcide. It is not just that these companies have been producing these products in response to demand. It is that they have conspired to create the demand in the first place, and then conspired further to keep the world dependent on fossil fuels. The oil companies, for example, together with automobile manufacturers, in the United States, prior to world war two, conspired to destroy the nation's mass transit system. In many cases, they simply bought up a city's trolley system, and then dismantled it. Railroads were passed over in favor of trucks. The nation became dependent on automobiles and trucks, and had to build a vast highway system, at public expense, to accommodate them, which led also to the creation of suburban America and malls, one of the most egregious patterns of human settlement ever built. The benefiting corporations had a heavy hand in all this. It didn't just happen naturally, accidentally. And now, for the past several decades, they have been vigorously conspiring to block the emergence of nonpolluting energy sources, like solar, wind, or thermal. These are enormously rich and powerful corporations, which spend millions in propaganda and in lobbying legislators the world over, to defeat efforts to deal with the problem of global warming by switching to clean energy.

So, what's going on here? Is this just greed? It's rather more complicated and considerably more evil. It's the profit-making system of capitalism functioning at its normal best. Entrepreneurs have always sought to use the state, from the dawn of capitalism, to gain competitive advantages for themselves. They have also always sought to externalize many of the costs of their operations. Oil companies are just doing what capitalist firms have always done, even though the consequences in this case are considerably more dire. It's not just about making money. It's about making money above all else, even life itself. It's about making money for themselves, no matter what the costs to others. That is, it's about making profit, and thus surviving as an actor in the system. Making profit comes to take precedence over all other human activities and desires. This is why it is said that 'the economy' dominates society (that is, the accumulators of capital do). And for the fossil fuel companies, making a profit even takes precedence over survival of a livable earth! The privileging of the profit-makers is inherent to the system, is deeply embedded, and cannot be eradicated by improving the moral quality of individuals. Private ownership of productive properties has to be abolished, as well as classes, and the state itself, and all of these replaced with cooperative, democratic social forms.

The problem is, and this is another complicating factor, that many of the people involved in these corporations, and the legislators who support them, believe their own propaganda. I believe there has always been a fairly large central core of hardheaded realists, who occupy positions of power and who set policy, or perhaps who are working behind the scenes, who do *not* believe the propaganda. These people see things as they are, see their enemies clearly, know exactly what they are doing and what the consequences will be, and know that their indictors are right, but who nevertheless go on being profit-mongers, and defending themselves in this, even with torture, assassination, and bombing. These are the truly evil people.

But for many, perhaps even the majority, of capitalists, they do not believe they are doing anything wrong. An ideology is not just to delude or brainwash the victims of a system. It is for the rulers too. It is an intellectual, moral, rational justification for what they are doing. It is only natural that they would believe it themselves, or most of them anyway. You cannot go through life knowing that you are a thief and a murderer and are very likely even destroying the earth and humanity with it. The truly evil can, and do, and are, but not ordinary persons. A big part of the job of radicals is to break through this ideological defense and convince these people that their actions are unconscionable. After that comes the problem of dealing with the profit-mongers who know this already but just don't give a damn.

I come now to a case that I finally have to admit is nothing but pure, unadulterated greed – the salaries of today's crop of corporate executives. The millions they are raking in is preposterous.

Is executive talent so hard to find that corporations have to pay millions to attract it? I don't think so. What's more likely is that these executives have gotten themselves into a position where they can write their own paychecks, with nobody around able or willing to stop them. Some of them are even getting sweetheart deals, worth millions, in severance pay, when they are being booted out of a company, after having run it into the ground. To the extent that these executives are suppressing wages or inflating prices so that they can bank millions, even if it means destroying the company they are supposed to be managing (by driving it into bankruptcy), unbridled greed appears to be motive. This is not even rational from the point of view of capitalists.

The current financial speculators working the stock markets of the world are another instance of greedy individuals gone berserk. These guys are rogues, basically, operating in recently deregulated financial markets (a deregulation engineered by the financial institutions themselves, but not I think to unleash rogue speculators). The speculators are not numerous, but they can move billions of dollars overnight, gambling with the futures of whole economies. I suspect that the financiers themselves will soon try to bring this aberration under control. In the meantime, we are witnessing the consuming sin of individual greed on a grand scale (or perhaps just a few addicted, criminal gamblers playing for extremely high stakes, at our expense).

But this is not the normal way of things under capitalism. The normal way is profit-making, by exploiting wage-slaves, and defending all the institutions needed to perpetuate this exploitation, through murder and war if need be. It is this system of exploitation that has to be undone, not just greed.

Capitalists have a choice of course. They don't have to keep doing this. They can stop being capitalists. They can give up profit-making and become wage-slaves. They can leave the ruling class and join the oppressed masses, and there have been some noted revolutionaries who have done just that. If capitalists become ashamed of what they are doing, they can certainly stop doing it. But if they remain capitalists, their behavior is prescribed: they have to make profits to survive, whether they are greedy or not.

One last caveat is necessary. The above analysis does not apply to nonprofit corporations. These corporations don't depend on profit-making for their survival, but on pleasing their sponsors or members, so that the grants or donations keep coming in. So it is a different dynamic entirely. The bloated salaries of some of the executives in many of these organizations would appear to be irrational and dysfunctional even from the point of view of the goals of the organization, because they siphon off resources and create stark inequalities of income within the organization, and hence reduce the effectiveness of the organization. This is hard to explain. But perhaps here the 'culture of greed', thrown up by the surrounding profit system, works as well as anything, facilitated of course by the inevitable hierarchies, salary differentials, upward mobility, and the whole sorry system. The fat salaries of many tenured professors probably fit into this category. I hope I have argued the point sufficiently well to persuade you.

4
A Stake, Not a Mistake: On Not Seeing the Enemy

October 2001

I spent several years in the early sixties studying Underdevelopment. It was frustrating, in that none of the theories I examined really seemed to explain the phenomenon. That is, the Theories of Development that were prevalent then (only in mainstream discourse, I later learned) didn't really answer the question: Why are some countries poor? I would look at US Aid programs, only to conclude that they didn't work, that they didn't help countries develop, and often got in the way. My response at that time was to argue, and to try to call to the attention of US Aid administrators, that the programs weren't working, and were not achieving the results they were supposed to. The programs were not facilitating development and economic growth in the countries they were supposed to be benefiting. Fortunately for me, with the explosion and re-emergence of radical consciousness in the late sixties, I was able to overcome this naiveté.

Unfortunately, though, for much of the American Left (especially for its so-called progressive wing), this naiveté, this bad habit of not seeing the enemy, this tendency to think that the US government's policies and actions are just mistakes, this seemingly ineradicable belief that the US government means well, is the most common outlook. It was certainly the predominant belief among those who opposed the Vietnam War. I helped write a broadsheet once, which we distributed at a big anti-war demonstration in Washington DC in November 1969, and which was titled "Vietnam is a Stake not a Mistake". In this document we spelled out the imperial reasons which explained why the government was waging war, quite deliberately and rationally, against Vietnam.

In subsequent decades there has been no end to the commentators who take the 'this is a mistake' line. Throughout the low intensity (i.e., terrorist) wars against Nicaragua and El Salvador in the 1980s we heard this complaint again and again. It is currently seen in the constant stream of commentaries on the US assault on Colombia. It has been heard repeatedly during the past two years in the demonstrations against the World Bank and the World Trade Organization. Protesters complain that the WTO's policies of structural adjustment are having the opposite effect of what they're supposed to. That is, they are hindering, not facilitating, development, and causing poverty, not alleviating it.

Two years ago, in 1999, throughout the 78 day bombing attack on Yugoslavia, much of the outpouring of progressive commentary on the event (that which didn't actually endorse the bombing that is) argued that "this is a mistake."[1] My favorite quote from that episode, was from Robert Hayden, Director of the Center for Russian and East European Studies at the University of Pittsburgh, being interviewed by Amy Goodman on *Democracy Now*, April 19, 1999. He said: "But we have the Clinton administration that developed a diplomacy that seems to have been intended to have produced this war, and now the Clinton administration's actions seem determined to produce

---

1 An excellent book on Yugoslavia which does not suffer from this naiveté, the best book so far, that I am aware of, on the bombing, is Michael Parenti, *To Kill a Nation: The Attack on Yugoslavia* (Verso, 2000, 246 pages).

a wider war." Amy Goodman: "Why would the Clinton Administration want to produce a war?" Hayden: "Boy, you know what? You've got me there. And as I say, you have to go back to the simple principles of incompetence. Never assume competence on the part of these guys." This was surely the bottom of the pit for the 'this is a mistake' crowd. I could cite quotes like this by the dozen, but instead let me turn to our current 'war'.

So, what has been the response of the 'progressive community' to the bombing of Afghanistan? As usual, they just don't get it. They just can't seem to grasp the simple fact that the government does this stuff on purpose. Endlessly, progressives talk as if the government is just making a mistake, does not see the real consequences of its actions, or is acting irrationally, and they hope to correct the government's course by pointing out the errors of its ways. Progressives assume that their goals – peace, justice, wellbeing – are also the government's goals. So when they look at what the government is doing, they get alarmed and puzzled, because it is obvious that the government's actions are not achieving these goals. So, they cry out: "Hey, this policy doesn't lead to peace!" or "Hey, this policy doesn't achieve justice (or democracy, or development)!" By pointing this out, they hope to educate the government, to help it to see its mistakes, to convince it that its policies are not having the desired results.[2]

How can they not see that the US government acts deliberately, and that it knows what it is doing? How can they not see that the government's goals are not peace and justice, but empire and profit. It *wants* these wars, this repression. These policies are not mistakes; they are not irrational; they are not based on a failure of moral insight (since morality is not even a factor in their considerations); they are not aberrations; they are not based on a failure

---

[2] Websites such as *Common Dreams* (www.commondreams.org), *Znet* (www.zmag.org/znet), and *Alternet* (www.alternet.org) are loaded with "this is a mistake" pieces, as are magazines like the *Nation*, the *Progressive*, *In These Times*, and the *Progressive Populist*.

to analyze the situation correctly; they are not based on ignorance. This repression, these bombings, wars, massacres, assassinations, and covert actions are the coldly calculated, rational, consistent, intelligent, and informed actions of a ruling class determined at all costs to keep its power and wealth and preserve its way of life (capitalism). It has demonstrated great historical presence, persistence, and continuity in pursuing this objective. This ruling class *knows* that it is committing atrocities, *knows* that it is destroying democracy, hope, welfare, peace, and justice, *knows* that it is murdering, massacring, slaughtering, poisoning, torturing, lying, stealing, and *it doesn't care.* Yet most progressives seem to believe that if only they point out often enough and loud enough that the ruling class is murdering people, that it will wake up, take notice, apologize, and stop doing it.

Here is a typical expression of this naiveté (written by an author, S. Brian Willson, who was in the process of introducing a list of US interventions abroad!):

> *Many of us are continually disturbed and grief stricken because it seems that our U.S. government does not yet understand: (a) the historical social, cultural, and economic issues that underlay most of the political and ecological problems of the world; (b) the need to comply with, as legally agreed to, rather than continually defy, international law and international institutions established for addressing conflict; and (c) that military solutions, including production, sale, and use of the latest in technological weapons, are simply ill-equipped and wrong-headed*

*for solving fundamental social and economic problems.*³

He is wrong on all three counts: (a) The US government has an intimate, detailed knowledge of the social, cultural, and economic characteristics of every country it intervenes in. It is especially familiar with the ethnic, linguistic, political, and religious divisions within the country. It is not interested in how these issues "underlay most of the political and ecological problems of the world", since it is not interested in those problems, certainly not in solving them, since it is the main creator of those problems. Rather, it uses its expert knowledge to manipulate events within the country in order to advance its own goals, profit and empire. (b) The US government understands perfectly that it expressly needs <u>not</u> to comply with international law in order to maintain its ability to act unilaterally, unfettered by any constraints, to advance its imperial aims. The claim that the US defies international law because of a misunderstanding is absurd. (c) Who says that the US government is trying to solve "fundamental social and economic problems?" These are not its aims at all. The objectives that it does pursue, consciously and relentlessly, namely profit and empire, are in fact the *causes* of these very "social and economic problems". Furthermore, for its true aims, military solutions, far from being "ill-equipped and wrongheaded," work exceptionally well. Military might sustain the empire. Arming every little client regime of the international ruling class with 'the latest in technological weapons" is necessary, and quite effective, in maintaining the repressive apparatus needed to defend empire, in addition to raking in lots of profit for the arms manufacturers. But evidently Mr. Willson "does not yet understand" any of

---

3 S. Brian Willson, "Who are the Real Terrorists? Why some veterans oppose counter- "terrorist" exercises", March 1999, Veterans for Peace, at: (www.mbay.net/~jenvic/vfp/mar22.htm).

Chapter 4

these things.

Let's take another example. Russell Mokhiber and Robert Weissman, otherwise very sensible writers, complain that "bombing a desperately poor country under the yoke of a repressive regime is a wrongheaded response [to the "unspeakable acts of violence" committed on Sept. 11]. "The U.S. bombing of Afghanistan should cease immediately," they say. They discuss three reasons: "1. The policy of bombing increases the risk of further terrorism against the United States. 2. The bombing is intensifying a humanitarian nightmare in Afghanistan. 3. There are better ways to seek justice." All three statements are true of course, but irrelevant, because seeking justice, avoiding humanitarian nightmares, and reducing the risk of terrorism do not enter into the calculations of US policy makers. Quite the contrary, US policy makers *create* injustice, humanitarian nightmares, and terrorism, throughout the world, in pursuit of the imperial objective of making profit, and this has been thoroughly documented in thousands of scholarly studies. So for Mokhiber and Weissman to talk in this way, and phrase the problem in this way, exposes their failure to really comprehend the enemy we face, which in turn prevents them from looking for effective strategies to defeat that enemy, like so many other opponents of the "war". Hence all the moralizing, the bulk of which is definitely directed at the rulers, not at the ruled. That is, it is not an attempt to win over the ruled, but an attempt to win over the rulers.[4]

It's what I call the "we should" crowd – all those people who hope to have a voice in the formation of policy, people whose stances are basically that of consultants to the ruling class. "We" should do this, "we" shouldn't do that, as if they had anything at all to say about what our rulers do. This is the normal stance among the bootlicking intelligen-

---

[4] Russell Mokhiber and Robert Weissman, "Three Arguments Against the War," posted on the *Common Dreams News Center* website for October 18, 2001 (www.commondreams.org).

tsia of course. But what is it doing among progressives and radicals? Even if their stance is seen to be not exactly that of consultants, but that of citizens making demands upon their government, what makes them think that the government ever listens? I think this attitude – the "we should" attitude – is rooted in part at least in the fact that most progressives still believe in nations and governments. They believe that this is "our" country, and that this is "our" government, or at least should be. So Kevin Danaher says that "we should get control of the government." They identify themselves as Americans, or Germans, or Mexicans, or Swedes. So they are constantly advising and making demands that 'their' government should do this and that. If they would reject nationalism altogether, and states and governments, they could begin to see another way.

A variation of the 'this is a mistake' theme has appeared in commentaries on the present "war", on Afghanistan. Progressives argue that the US is "falling into a trap". They argue that Osama bin Laden had hoped to provoke the US into doing just what it is doing, attacking Afghanistan. In their view, the US government is being stupid, acting blindly, responding irrationally, and showing incompetence. That is, it is "making a mistake". It never seems to occur to these analysts that the government may actually be awake, even alert, or that it jumped at the opportunity offered it by the attacks of September 11 to do what it had wanted to do anyway – seize Afghanistan, build a big new base in Uzbekistan, declare unending war on the enemies of Empire everywhere, and initiate draconian repression against internal dissent in order to achieve "domestic tranquility".

I saw yet another variation on the theme just recently. John Tirman writes about "Unintended Consequences."[5] He thinks that "No matter how cautious generals and political leaders are ... unseen and unintended [results] occur,

---

5 John Tirman, "Unintended Consequences", posted on *Alternet*, Oct 24, 2001 (at www.alternet.org).

at times as a bitter riptide which overwhelms the original rationales for engaging in armed combat. This unpredictable cycle of action and reaction has thwarted U.S. policy in southwest Asia for 50 years." It's the usual mistake: Tirman imputes policies to the US government which it does not have. US policy has not been thwarted, it has been highly successful. The US has succeeded in keeping control of Middle Eastern oil for the past half century. This is what it wanted to do, and this is what it did. Tirman however reviews the history of US intervention in the Middle East, beginning with the overthrow of Mosaddegh in Iran in 1953, and sees it as one long blunder, nothing but bumbling incompetence, complicated further by 'unintended consequences' which thwart the goals of American foreign policy. He seems to think that the US was (or "should be") trying to reduce US dependence on Middle Eastern oil, fighting Islamic fundamentalism, reducing human suffering, assisting in economic development, promoting democracy, and so on − anything and everything except what it is actually doing, keeping control of Middle Eastern oil, and using any means necessary to do so. Tirman is aware of course that this (oil) is the true aim of US policy, because he quotes directly from US officials who state this objective explicitly, but somehow this doesn't sink in. Instead, he finally asks in exasperation: "What will be next in this series of haunting mistakes?"

Ariel Dorfman, author of a creative critique of US imperialism, in the form of *How to Read Donald Duck: Imperialist Ideology in the Disney Comic*, was being interviewed on *Democracy Now* by Amy Goodman, on October 25, 2001, about the assassination of Digna Ochoa, the leading civil rights lawyer in Mexico. When asked by Goodman to put the murder in the larger context of what was happening in the world, like in Afghanistan, Dorfman replied: "Because the US is in Afghanistan and it needs all its allies behind it, they are going to turn a blind eye to all the abuses of authority that are happening." Pardon me? A blind eye?

Isn't the US government in the business, with both eyes open, of murdering labor leaders, leftists, progressives, and civil rights activists all over the world? Dorfman went on to say that now would be "a good moment that President Bush could call his friend Vicente Fox and say: 'I want the murderers of Digna Ochoa put on trial'." Excuse me! Is he kidding? It's quite probable that Bush did call Fox, but with a rather different message, namely, to tell him that while the world's attention was focused on Afghanistan, now would be a good time to kill Digna Ochoa y Plácido.

An Afghani man from Kabul escaped into Pakistan carrying a packet of letters addressed to the world's leaders, "handwritten messages from his panic-stricken community."

"The world must know what is happening in Afghanistan," said Mohammed Sardar, 46, his voice ragged with anxiety and anger. "The terrorists and the leaders are still free, but the people are dying and there is no one to listen to us. I must get to President Bush and the others and tell them they are making a terrible mistake."[6]

The widespread belief that the US government has good intentions, a belief held onto tenaciously in spite of decades of overwhelming empirical evidence refuting it, has got to be one of the greatest phenomena of mass delusion in history. It would take a twenty-first century Freud to unravel this one. Here is a government that has already bombed two other countries to smithereens just in the past ten years, first Iraq and then Yugoslavia (not to mention endless interventions abroad since its inception).[7] Now it is

---

[6] Reported by Pamela Constable, *Washington Post*, Oct 24, 2001, "Plaintive Afghan's Plea from Community: Stop the Bombing".

[7] The best brief introduction to this history that I have seen so far is "A Concise History of United States Global Interventions, 1945 to Present," by William Blum, in his *Rogue State: A Guide to the World's Only Superpower* (Common Courage, 2000, 308 pages), pp. 125-162. References to longer lists of interventions covering the whole history of the U.S. government can be found in Zoltan Grossman's "One Hundred Years of Intervention," on *Jay's Leftist and Progressive Internet Resource Directory* (www.neravt.com/left/invade.htm). See also, Steve Kangas, "A Timeline of CIA Atrocities," available on the

Chapter 4

bombing Afghanistan to smithereens – hospitals, fuel supplies, food depots, electrical systems, water systems, radio stations, telephone exchanges, remote villages, mosques, old folks' homes, UN offices, Red Cross warehouses, clinics, schools, neighborhoods, roads, dams, airports – and a victim of the assault escapes to plead for help from the very people who are attacking him. To have created such an illusion as this is surely one of the greatest feats of propaganda ever seen.[8]

So although it is important to try to shatter this illusion, it is ultimately not enough, and of very limited effectiveness, simply to list all the atrocities committed by our rulers, carefully expose all their double standards, accuse them of being the real terrorists, morally condemn what they are doing, or call for peace. All these arguments are useful of course in the battle for the hearts and minds of average people, *if average people ever heard them*, which they do not, for the most part. And if they do hear them, it's like they (most of them) are tuning in to madness, they're so brainwashed. It takes a lot more than mere arguments to break through the mindset of a thoroughly indoctrinated people.

Of all the dozens of comments that I read on the government's response to the attacks of September Eleven, precious few raised the key question: How do we stop them (the government, from attacking Afghanistan)? For the

---

Liberalism Resurgent website at (http://home.att.net/~Resurgence/CIAtimeline.html).

8 The only other essay from this deluge of writing about the so-called war on terrorism that I have seen which challenges the 'this is a mistake' line (although many people have pointed out that the US government is itself a terrorist state), is a really excellent piece by Edward Herman and David Peterson, "Who Terrorizes Whom?", posted on *Zmag* website, dated October 18, 2001 (www.zmag.org/whoterrorizes.htm). In discussing Richard Falk's claim that the attack on Afghanistan is "the first truly just war since World War II", for example, they write: "it never occurs to Falk that the right-wing Republican regime of Bush and Cheney, so close to the oil industry and military-industrial complex, might have an agenda incompatible with a just war." They call this Left Accommodationism, cite several examples, and give a good analysis of the phenomenon.

most part, progressive commentators don't even raise questions of strategy.⁹ They are too busy analyzing ruling class ideology, in order to highlight its hypocrisies. Proving that the ruling class is hypocritical doesn't get us very far. It's useful of course. Doing this work is an important task. Noam Chomsky, for example, devotes himself almost exclusively to this task, and we should be thankful that we have his research. He usually does mention also, somewhere in almost every speech, article, or interview, that 'it doesn't have to be this way', that this situation we are in is not inevitable, and that we can change it. But when asked "How?", he replies, "Organize, agitate, educate." Well, sure. But the Christian Coalition organizes, agitates, and educates. So did the Nazis and the Klu Klux Klan. The Taliban organizes, agitates, and educates. So does the ruling class, and it does so in a massive and highly successful way, which results in overwhelming hegemony for its point of view.

In spite of more than three decades of blistering exposés of US foreign policy, and in spite of the fact that he is an anarchist, and is thus supposedly against all government, at least in the long run, Chomsky still regularly uses the 'universal we'. Much of the time Chomsky says "The US government does this, or does that," but some of the time he says "We do this, or we do that," thus including himself, and us, as agents in the formation and execution of US foreign policy. This is an instance of what I call the 'universal we'. It presumes a democracy that does not exist. The average American has no say whatsoever in the formation and execution of US foreign policy. Nor do we even have any influence in picking the people who are making it, since we have no say over who gets to run for office or what they do after they are elected. So, to say something like "_we_ shouldn't be bombing Afghanistan", as so many progres-

---

9 A rare exception is Naomi Klein, who frequently focuses on questions of strategy. See for example, "Signs of the Times," the *Nation*, October 22, 2001.

sives do, is highly misleading, and expresses a misperception and misdiagnosis of the situation we are in.

In the question period following Chomsky's major address on "The New War Against Terror" (delivered at MIT on October 18),[10] Chomsky was challenged by a man in the audience who accused Chomsky of blaming America for the tragedy of September 11. Chomsky correctly said that the term America is an abstraction and cannot do anything. But then he said that he blamed himself, and his questioner, and others present, for this event (implying that 'we' are responsible for what 'our' government does). This is a half-truth at best. The blame for September 11 rests squarely on those who did it. Next, to the extent that a connection can be proved between their actions and US foreign policy, the US government is to blame, and the ruling class that controls the government. Average Americans are to blame for what the US government does only in the sense that they have not managed to change or block its policies, either because they haven't tried or because they have tried but have failed.

Of course, the category of Average American is an abstraction as well. Many average Americans vigorously support US foreign policy. Others oppose it, but have failed to change it. Those of us who want a real democracy, and want to put an end to Empire, have so far failed to do so, and only in this sense are we in anyway responsible for September Eleven. But even this failure must be judged in light of the relative strengths that the parties bring to the fight. We cannot fault ourselves for being defeated by an opponent with overwhelmingly superior forces, as long as we fought as bravely and as hard as we could. Our task is to find ways to enhance our strengths and weaken theirs. To

---

[10] The transcript of this speech has been posted on *Znet*. The speech was broadcast on *Democracy Now* (www.webactive.com/pacifica/exile) on October 23 and 24, 2001. A tape recording of the speech is also available for purchase from *Alternative Radio* (www.alternative-radio.org). Streaming audio is also available on(www.zmag.org/znet/GlobalWatch/chomskymit.htm).

fail to make a distinction between the ruling class and the rest of us hinders this task, causes us to presume a democracy that does not exist, to misunderstand exactly what we are up against, and to misidentify the enemy. It thus prevents us from devising a successful strategy for defeating this enemy.

In this same speech, which was over an hour long, Chomsky didn't once mention oil. When questioned about this during the discussion that followed, he said that of course oil was always there in the background, for anything happening in the Middle East, but he didn't see oil as an immediate factor in the current crisis. He is surely wrong about this. There is plenty of evidence that securing Afghanistan, in order to get a pipeline through to the Arabian Sea, is a key consideration for US policy makers. They are already in the process of building a huge new military base in Uzbekistan (just as they are building one in Kosovo), and have concluded a long-term agreement with the Uzbekistan government to do so, similar to ones they have made in Saudi Arabia, Spain, Turkey, Philippines, and elsewhere. These bases will be used to secure the Central Asian oil and gas reserves for the West. They will also be thrown into service to accomplish another aim, beyond oil, namely, to facilitate the recolonization of the Balkans and Russia, and to ensure that they do not return to Communism or try to escape the New World Order. This is the larger geopolitical objective that drives the Empire builders.

Howard Zinn seems to think it is all a struggle between an 'old way of thinking', based on war and violence, and a 'new way of thinking' based on peace and nonviolence. Hardly a hint here of Empire, and no hint at all of Profit and Capital. As moving and inspiring as his remarks were on the September Eleven crisis[11] they just didn't cut it, as

---

11 Howard Zinn's initial remarks on the September Eleven tragedy were aired on *Democracy Now* on September 13, 2001 in an interview with Amy Goodman (www.webactive/pacifica/exile). Zinn made similar remarks in an interview with Noelle Hanrahan on *Flashpoints*

concerns getting ourselves out of the horrible situation we are in. Zinn of course it very aware (but most so-called progressives aren't) of ruling classes, empire, capital, and profit, and has labored long and hard to write their histories and people's opposition to them. But somehow this doesn't get reflected in his thinking about what to do about it all now. When it comes to strategy, moral condemnation is where he rested his case, in his response to these events at least.

In a speech on October 21, in Burlington, Vermont, Zinn said that we must change from being a military superpower to being a moral superpower.[12] During the speech he had vividly described the many foreign invasions undertaken by the US government and their devastating consequences, claimed that America was not a peaceful nation, reminded us that governments lie, pointed out that oil is the key to American foreign policy in the Middle East, and described the vast deployment of military bases and armament all over the world in order to extend American power. He may even have mentioned profit once or twice. But he never once mentioned 'capitalism' (let alone 'colonialism', 'imperialism', or 'ruling class'), nor did he in any way indicate an awareness that the projection of American power all over the world is for a reason, that it is being used in defense of a particular social order, and that this social order benefits, and is therefore being defended by, a particular class.

It's almost as if Zinn thinks that the US government could simply pack up and go home, if it only wanted to – dismantle its bases, pull its armies, fleets, and planes out, and leave the world alone. If the US ruling class did that, it, and the system upon which it feeds, capitalism, would

---

Radio on September 13, 2001 (www.flashpoints.net). A short essay along the same lines was published in *The Progressive*, for November, 2001, "The Old Way of Thinking", pp. 8-9.

[12] Howard Zinn's speech in Burlington, Vermont on October 21, 2001 was broadcast on *Democracy Now* on Oct 22, 2001 (www.webactive/pacifica/exile). A tape recording of the speech is also available for purchase from *Alternative Radio* (www.alternativeradio.org).

collapse. So we know that it is not going to dismantle its forward bases and leave the world alone, no matter how hard we try to shame it with our moralizing. Zinn did not seem to grasp this fact or to recognize that there is an enemy that has to be defeated, before the $350 billion could be taken away from the Pentagon and used to help people (another one of his recommendations). And when it came time to talk about what to do about it all, he recommended organizing demonstrations and writing letters to our congressional representatives!

The 'peace now' protesters strike a similar stance. Of course, it was heartening to see an anti-war movement blossom almost immediately. But it was also disheartening. It meant that radicals were letting the warmongers set the agenda. Instead of continuing the fight against neoliberalism and its institutions, and against capitalism, oppositionists suddenly dropped all this to launch an anti-war campaign. The candlelight vigils, especially, seemed to me a pathetic response to a war-mongering, repressive government. This happens again and again. The government launches a war of aggression, and the peaceniks take to the streets, with their candles, crying "peace now" and "no more war". Do they ever win? Have they ever stopped even one war? Do they ever even think about how they could win? Doesn't the inefficacy of their response prove that they are not really serious about peace? Do they ever think about ways of actually stopping the murderers rather than just pleading with them not to kill? They keep saying that peace cannot be achieved by going to war. Who says the US government wants peace!? They quote A.J. Muste as saying that war is not the way to peace; peace is the way. Is this relevant? Does it make sense to quote such thoughts to a government that has always engaged, from its inception two hundred years ago, in systematic mass murder?

Similarly, with the bulk of the other progressive commentators. They are just trying to change the government's policy, not stop them and deprive them of power.

Chapter 4

Here is a typical sentence. Rahul Mahajan and Robert Jensen write: "The next step is for us to build a movement that can change our government's barbaric and self-destructive policy."[13] You see, from the government's point of view, its policy is not barbaric or self-destructive. It is intelligent, self-serving, and self-preserving. Mahajan and Jensen actually pretty much admit this in their piece, by reasoning that "This war is about the extension of U.S. power. It has little to do with bringing the terrorists to justice, or with vengeance." (Such a view is rather rare among progressives actually.) They argue that there are three other motives for the war, from the government's point of view: the desire to defend "imperial credibility", to control "oil and natural gas of Central Asia," and "to push a right-wing domestic agenda." Nevertheless, in spite of these insights, they still stop short of realizing that they therefore have to fight, stop, and neutralize the government, rather than just change its policy. Given who the government is, who it serves (capital, the rich), and what its interests and priorities are, it can't change its policies into those favored by progressives, not and survive as an imperial power that is.

It is not only as regards foreign policy that the 'this is a mistake' line makes an appearance. Progressive commentators suffer from this affliction with regards to domestic policy too. If the government passes a tax cut to benefit the richest corporations and super rich individuals, but calls it a package to stimulate the economy, progressives complain loudly that the bill doesn't accomplish what it's supposed to, that it doesn't stimulate the economy. Why can't they simply admit that the government (the Administration *and* Congress) *intended* and *wanted* to give more money to the rich ruling class, because it is from, and represents the interests of, this class, and that it called its bill an economic stimulus package only in order to sell it and to deceive

---

[13] Rahul Mahajan and Robert Jensen, "A War of Lies", posted on the *Common Dreams News Center* website for October 8, 2001 (www.commondreams.org).

the American public?

The 'this is a mistake' crowd was out in full force in the discussion surrounding the new anti-terrorist legislation which the Bush Administration submitted to Congress immediately after the September Eleven attacks. Attorney General Ashcroft said that the government had taken pains not to abridge any of our precious civil rights in its efforts to deal with the terrorist threat, and had tried to strike a balance between security and liberty. So progressives took him at his word and started pointing out that this wasn't true, that the bill did step on our civil rights and did not strike a good balance between security and liberty. Then they started coming up with a bunch of excuses. They said the bill was 'rammed through Congress'. Well, why did Congress permit this? They said the leaders of Congress bypassed the usual rules and procedures, and dealt with the bill basically in secret? Well, if Congress is committed to democracy, why can't it practice democracy in its own halls? And why weren't there attempts to stop this secret handling of the bill? They said that Congress didn't even have a chance to read the bill. Well, why didn't it take the time to do so, and delay the vote until it had?

This bill, the so-called USA Patriot Act of 2001, which shreds the fourth amendment (protection against unwarranted search and seizure), gives the government the right to spy on everyone, bypasses criminal law, the courts, and due process in numerous instances, plus dozens more horrors, was passed in the Senate by a vote of 98-1. So this flaming liberal senator, Edward Kennedy, didn't realize what he was voting for? Please. He knew. They knew. *And they wanted it.* The Administration and Congress (minus 66 representatives in the House and 1 senator in the Senate) were united in their desire to further strengthen the Police State that they have been building for some time. They are not committed to democracy. They are committed to preserving capitalism, which is their lifeblood. You think they haven't noticed the growing protest movement

Chapter 4

that has erupted onto the world scene in the last two years? You think they're not worried about that movement and determined to stop it?

A friendly, tolerant, enlightened, pseudo-democratic capitalism is no longer historically feasible (not that it was ever really much of any of these things). We are living in the age of Zero Tolerance Capitalism, with its Global War Machine, its Mammoth Intelligence Agencies, its Secret Police, its Echelons and Carnivores, its Covert Operations, its humongous Police Departments, its ubiquitous Security Guards, its Death Squads, its National Security States, its Swat Teams and Special Forces, its State Terrorism and Torture, its High-Tech Surveillance, its Non-Lethal Weapons, its Low-Intensity Warfare, its Para-Militaries, its Mercenaries, its Smart Bombs, its Prison-Industrial Complex, its Chemical, Biological, and Nuclear weapons, and its World Bank and World Trade Organization. Now, with the US Congress's aptly-named USA Patriot Act of 2001, it has finally managed to shred the Bill of Rights. The US ruling class never wanted the Bill of Rights to begin with; it was forced on them.

So the Hitlers and Mussolinis of the world have won after all (almost). All the while we were thinking that we had rid the world of fascism in the Second World War, fascism was sneaking in the back door, and turning America into a World Fascist Empire. Zero Tolerance fascist-like regimes, supported and often installed by the United States, have long existed throughout most of the world – Mobutu in Zaire, Pinochet in Chile, Somoza in Nicaragua, Armas in Guatemala, Franco in Spain, Papadopoulos in Greece, Pahlavi in Iran, Marcos in the Philippines, Sharon in Israel. Now the repressive, Zero Tolerance, National Security State, has come home to America. They will probably start torturing and killing in Europe and America the way they have been doing everywhere else. (They are already torturing and killing, but they have managed so far to keep it under wraps). Will they get away with it?

How many centuries of mass murder does it take to prove that ruling classes dependent on and devoted to a system based on profit are impervious to moral appeal, and are beyond redemption, certainly as long as they have any power left to continue killing? Moral appeals are useless against such people. Were moral appeals enough to defeat the Nazis, and German and Italian Fascism? Didn't we have to fight them? Similarly, with our current warmongers and empire builders, with American Fascism, if you will. They must be faced with real opposition, although not necessarily military opposition, which actually is not even an option for us, given that it is so impossible for poor people to acquire the weapons. It is thus ineffective to even think about fighting a war in traditional terms, as this is not a possible, nor a winning, strategy. All the same, the rulers' power to exploit, oppress, murder, and wage war must be destroyed. We need to come up with a strategy for doing this. It certainly cannot be done merely by taking to the streets, holding candlelight vigils, or exposing their hypocrisy. The war must be fought, to be sure, but fought in new ways, ways that are within our means and that can lead to victory.

The Urgent Need to Reassemble Ourselves to Take Power Away from Criminals.

I believe that there is a way to defeat this global ruling class, but it means that we have to reassemble ourselves socially on a massive scale. We have to gather ourselves together in directly democratic, face-to-face deliberative assemblies at work, at home, and in our neighborhoods. This would give us a foundation from which to begin draining power and wealth away from the ruling class. Without these social forms, we are necessarily restricted to all the various forms of reformism, restricted to trying to work through NGOs or state and national governments, to changing ruling class behavior, to making moral appeals, or to seeking to get or reverse certain legislation. But by reorganizing ourselves into a multitude of small, decentralized, directly democratic, face-to-face, local assemblies, coalesced together into inter-regional associations by means of voluntary treaties, we can begin to take back control of our lives and communities, and get the ruling class off our backs.

I have sketched out this strategy in my book *Getting Free*,[14] and have discussed there in some detail its various implications. As long as the world is organized on the basis of governments and corporations, nations and profit, there will never be peace, justice, freedom, or democracy. Our task is nothing less than to get rid of the social order we live in, and to create another one to take its place. If we fail to do this now, we will shortly find ourselves living in a full-fledged world fascist empire a thousand times more powerful and sophisticated than the Nazis ever could have been, and from which it will be next to impossible to escape.

Further Reading on Selected Topics

On US Interventions Abroad
William Blum, *Killing Hope: U.S. Military and CIA Interventions since World War II* (Common Courage, 1995, 457 pages).

On Terrorism
Edward S. Herman, *The Real Terror Network: Terrorism in Fact and Propaganda* (South End Press, 1982, 252 pages).

On Fascism

---

14 James Herod, *Getting Free: Creating an Association of Democratic Autonomous Neighborhoods* (2007) is available from AK Press.

David McGowan, *Understanding the F-Word: American Fascism and the Politics of Illusion* (iUniverse, 2001, 276 pages).

Patriot Act
Analyses of the USA Patriot Act of 2001 can be found on the websites of the American Civil Liberties Union (wwwaclu.org) and the Electronic Frontier Foundation (www.eff.org).

On Fundamentalism
Fotis Terzakis, "Irrationalism, Fundamentalism, and Religious Revival: The Colors of the Chess-Board," *Democracy and Nature*, Vol. 4, Nos. 2/3 (Issue 11/12, no date, but c.1998), also available on the Internet at: (www.democracynature.org/dn/vol4/terzakis_irrationalism.htm).
Colin Ward, "Fundamentalism", *The Raven*, No. 27 (Freedom Press) on the Net at (www.ecn.org/freedom/ Raven/fund.html).
Frederick Clarkson, *Eternal Hostility: The Struggle between Theocracy and Democracy* (Common Courage, 1996, 277 pages).

On Empire
Michael Parenti, *Against Empire* (City Lights, 1995, 216 pages).
Peter Gowan, *The Global Gamble: Washington's Faustian Bid for World Dominance* (Verso, 1999, 230 pages).
Michael Hardt and Antonio Negri, *Empire* (Harvard University Press, 2001, 478 pages).
Joseph Gerson and Bruce Birchard, editors, *The Sun Never Sets: Confronting the Network of Foreign U.S. Military Bases* (South End Press, 1991, 389 pages).

Chapter 4

On Afghanistan
A few of the better essays on the attack on Afghanistan, which for the most part don't make the mistake of thinking that the US government doesn't know what it's doing, are (all dates are from 2001): Alexander Cockburn and Jeffrey St Clair, "Bush's Wars", *Counterpunch*, Sept 21 (plus many more fine essays on this crisis by these authors posted on *Counterpunch* website: www.counterpunch.org); John Pilger, "Hidden Agenda Behind War on Terror," *Mirror* /UK, October 29 (plus many other excellent essays, at http://pilger.carlton.com/print); Michel Chossudovsky, "Osamagate," (posted October 9, at www.globalresearch.ca/articles/ CHO110A.print.html); Francis A. Boyle, "No War Against Afghanistan!," Oct 18 (msanews.nynet.net/Scholars/Boyle/nolwar.html); Edward Said, "The Clash of Ignorance," the *Nation*, October 22; Sitaram Yechury, "America, Oil, and Afghanistan," *The Hindu*, October 13; Edward S. Herman, "Antiterrorism as a Cover for Terrorism," (www.zmag.org/ hermancover.html); Arundhati Roy, "War Is Peace," *Outlook*, Oct. 18 (later published in the *Guardian*, Oct 23); Sunera Thobani, "War Frenzy," (www.neravt.com/left/thobani.html); Michael Parenti, "Terrorism Meets Reactionism," (www.michaelparenti.org/Terrorism.html); George Monbiot, "America's Pipe Dream," *Guardian* /UK, Oct 23); Jared Israel, Rick Rozoff & Nico Varkevisser, "Why Washington Wants Afghanistan," (posted Sept 18, on www.emperors- clothes.com/analysis/afghan.htm); Sean Healy, "The Empire wants war, not justice," (no date, www.zmag.org/healywar.htm); Noam Chomsky, "The New War Against Terror," Oct 18 (www.zmag.org/GlobalWatch/chomskymit.htm); Patrick Martin, "US-Uzbekistan pact sheds light on Washington's war aims in Central Asia," *World Socialist Website* (www.wsws.org/articles/2001/oct2001/uzbe-o18_pm.shtml); Nick Beams, "Behind the 'anti-terrorism' mask: imperialist powers prepare new forms of colonialism," *World Socialist Website*, Oct 18 (www.wsws.org/articles/2001/oct2001/

imp-o18_pm.shtml); Vijay Prashad, "War against the Planet," (no date, www.zmag.org/prashcalam.htm); Stan Goff, "The So-Called Evidence is a Farce," October 10, *Narco News* (www.narconews.com/ goff1.html); Al Giordano, "Washington's 'Terrorist' List: Road through Afghanistan leads to Colombia," Oct 1, *Narco News, A-Info News Service* Al-Ahram, 18-24 October (www.ahram.org/eg/weekly/2001/556/op9); Renfrey Clarke, "War on terrorism or war on the Third World?, *Green Left*, Oct 17 (www.greenleft.org.au/current/ 467p16.htm); Robin Blackburn, "Road to Armageddon," *Counterpunch*, Oct 3. All website addresses valid as of October, 2001. (www.narconews.com/war2.html); Chicago Area Anarchists, "Anarchists against the expansion of capitalism and the war," (www.infoshop.org/inews/stories.php?story=01/10/25/7453849); Jared Israel, "Washington Plots, Moscow Crawls, Kabul Burns," (www.emperors-clothes.com/misc/burns); Hani Shukrallah, "Capital Strikes Back," (www.neravt.com/left).

The following websites have extensive links covering September Eleven, Afghanistan, and the so-called war on terrorism: *Common Dreams News Center* (www.commondreams.org), *Znet* (www.zmag.org/znet.htm), *Jay's Leftist and Progressive Internet Directory, Alternet* (www.alternet.org), *Counterpunch* (www.counterpunch.org), *Mid-Atlantic Info Shop* (www.infoshop.org/news); *Global Circle Net News* (www.globalcircle.net).

This essay was published in the **Anarcho Syndicalist Review**, *#34, Spring 2002.*

5
Abolish the Stock Market: A Brief Diagnosis of the Depression
(Being mostly a survey of scholarly research)

March 2009

It is obscene and insane that a few ten thousand very rich persons (multi-millionaires and billionaires) can, by placing bets (gambling) in the world's stock exchanges (casinos), artificially jack up, within months, the price of rice, wheat, corn, and other food staples, thus forcing a billion or more people to the very edge of starvation. Obviously, such an abominable situation should not exist.

So you'd think there would be a great clamor to abolish the stock market. But then, you'd think that there would be a clamor to abolish the CIA also, which is an absolute evil, and the Pentagon, an equally absolute evil, as well as Hollywood. But as big and bad as these outfits are they are nothing compared to the biggest abomination of them all – capitalism, including its nation-state system. (While we're in the abolishing mode, let's abolish money, which would get rid of all these evil institutions in one fell swoop.)

The current financial meltdown we're in is just an artifact of capitalism, and it certainly can't be explained with-

Chapter 5

out taking this system into account, although plenty of people are trying to do just that. The most popular explanation says that those Wall Street bankers are just *too damned greedy.*

So what's going on? I have pieced together the following sketch of the crisis from the writings of our radical social philosophers and historians who have studied the matter, scholars such as John Bellamy Foster and Fred Magdoff, most importantly, but also Immanuel Wallerstein, Michael Hudson, Michel Chossudovsky, Doug Henwood, and Silvia Federici / George Caffentzis, among many others.

To begin with, we are in the early stages of a major depression. This is not a typical brief recession, but a deep, long-lasting, systemic, global depression. It may last a decade. There will be massive unemployment. Hundreds of thousands of businesses will go bankrupt. Maybe a hundred thousand nongovernmental organizations will shut down for lack of funding. Millions will lose their homes. Millions more will lose their pensions. Malls will stand deserted. Poverty will increase dramatically. Millions more people will starve to death in the poorer countries.

A depression is when the so-called economy contracts significantly, maybe by as much as 10-15%. That is, "growth" stops. Growth of what? Capital accumulation. Capital cannot find ways to continue to expand. That is, rich people cannot find ways to invest their surplus money which will yield sufficient profit. When the rate of profit falters, crisis ensues. General panic sets in amongst "investors" (people who make money off money). Capitalism – a system for accumulating capital for the sake of accumulating capital – requires incessant growth (new products, new markets), which is why it is often likened to a cancer, and why it must be eradicated.

As it happened, capitalism has a cyclical aspect. It grows for thirty years or so and then stagnates for roughly thirty more years, with the cycle ending in a depression. And so it has been for five hundred years. The years of stagnation stem from the increasing difficulty of keeping the rate of profit up through the production of goods and services. The built-up productive capacity outstrips demand. If goods and services don't sell, no profit can be realized, and there is no point in making further investments in the "real economy." So the people who own surplus capital shift over to financial speculation in an effort to keep the profits flowing in. This process is entirely normal to the system.

This is what has been happening again recently. There was a stagnating economy combined with an over-abundance of capital with nowhere to go, so the rich turned to gambling, in a rigged game which yielded enormous profits for a while to those in the know. But now the casino has gone belly up, the system has crashed, and a depression has commenced.

Historically, after a depression, the cycle starts over again. There is some disagreement among radical scholars, however, as to whether the cycle will restart this time in the usual way and continue on as before. Wallerstein, for example, believes that capitalism has reached barriers to its continued growth which it will not be able to overcome and that the system will be gone within twenty to forty years. Most analysts do not go this far, some even claiming that the idea that capitalism will self-destruct is nonsense.

There is general agreement though that the current crisis has distinctive features which make it different from all preceding ones. For one thing, there is the sheer volume of the surplus capital that is sloshing around the world looking for "investment opportunities." We're talking about tens of trillions of dollars, much of it changing hands overnight. Also, with high-speed computers, million-dollar bets can be placed which last only a few minutes. Very little of this betting now takes place in the stock market per se. Most of it is done in the commodity, bond, and currency markets, and through over the counter betting.

Plus, in recent years, the gamblers have invented a whole basketful of new ways to bet (called "financial instru-

Chapter 5

ments," e.g., derivatives – forwards, futures, options, swaps, collars). For example, they can bet that the prices of currencies, commodities, or stocks will rise or fall. Much of the spike in the price of oil last year was caused by betting. Millions of dollars worth of bets that the value of a company's stock will fall can then become a self-fulfilling prophecy, and a perfectly normal profit-earning company can be destroyed. Gamblers can buy insurance to cover the risks of their bets, and then bet on the ability of the insurance company to pay. These practices strike any normal person as total madness, but they are completely rational from the point of view of the financial elite, who will grab profit any which way they can.

In recent years, in the United States, the financial wing of the capitalist ruling class, which is now predominant, has further compounded the madness by getting rid of all government regulations over its activities. It has gotten the situation back to pre-World War I days when the Robber Barons had a completely free hand to do any damned thing they wanted to, the result being the Great Depression of 1929. So the Roosevelt wing of the ruling class stepped in, back then, to save capitalism from itself with the watered-down USAmerican version of the welfare state – the New Deal. This is not likely to happen again, because there is no massive socialist movement to exert pressure from below, nor is the ruling class as divided. Capitalists have never been in such complete control of everything as they now are in the United States. They face no serious opposition.

What is the likely outcome of all this? We can see from the government's response to the crisis so far. All steps taken to date serve to cover the losses of the financial elite (wealthy gamblers). They get to keep the profits they made when the betting was good, and then have the government, using general tax revenue, cover their losses after the betting tanked. This does not mean that the banks are being nationalized. Quite the contrary. It is the privatization of the government. Wall Street has simply taken over the US

Treasury Department.

The end result will be the further concentration of capital into fewer very powerful corporations, and the further consolidation of ruling class power.

Anarchists can use this crisis to discredit capitalism and organize campaigns to dismantle it. A good beginning is the emerging Boycott Banks campaign. (See information at: <http://www.bankstrike.net/organizing-financial-crisis>.)

This essay was published in **BAAM**, *#19, March 2009, the newsletter of the Boston Anti-Authoritarian Movement.*

Recommended Reading

On the Financial Meltdown
Foster, John Bellamy, and Fred Magdoff, *The Great Financial Crisis* (Monthly Review Press, February 2009, 160 pages). This is the best radical analysis of the crisis so far.
Immanuel Wallerstein, "The Depression: A Long-Term View," October 8, 2008, at: <http://www.binghamton.edu/fbc/243en.htm>. See also the long interview with Wallerstein by Jae-Jung Suh, "Capitalism's Demise?" January 10, 2009, online at: <http://english.hani.co.kr/popups/print.hani?ksn=332037>.
Michael Hudson. A convenient archive of Hudson's essays on the crisis can be found at: <http://www.globalresearch.ca/>. Go to their author index, click on H, and scroll down to Hudson.
Michel Chossudovsky, "America's Fiscal Collapse," March 2, 2009, online at:

<http://www.globalresearch.ca/index.
php?context=va&aid=12517>.
Doug Henwood, "Reflections on the Current Crisis – Part Two," *Left Business Observer* #118, April 2008, online at: <http://www.leftbusinessobserver.com/Turmoil2.html>.
There is a link to Part One.
Silvia Federici and George Caffentzis, "Notes on the Wall Street Meltdown," October 10, 2008, online at: <http://freeofstate.org/new/?p=4208>.
Peter Gowan, "Crisis in the Heartland," *New Left Review*, #55, January-February 2009, online at: <http://www.newleftreview.org/?page=article&view=2759>.
David Harvey, "Why the U.S. Stimulus Package is Bound to Fail," February 13, 2009, online at: <http://www.zmag.org/znet/viewArticle/20559>. See also Harvey's March 13/15, 2009 essay on Counterpunch, "The Crisis and the Consolidation of Class Power: Is This Really the End of Neoliberalism?" online at: <http://www.counterpunch.org/harvey03132009.html>.
Leo Panitch and Sam Gindin, "From Global Finance to the Nationalization of the Banks: Eight Theses on the Economic Crisis," February 25, 2009 online at: <http://www.globalresearch.ca/index.php?context=va&aid=12463>.
See also an interview with Panitch, February 18, 2009, at:
<http://zcommunications.org/znet/viewArticlePrint/20602>.
Paul Bowman, "Financial Weapons of Mass Destruction," September 2008, online at:

<http://www.anarkismo.net/article/9850?print_page=true>.

Matt Taibbi, "The Big Takeover," *Rolling Stone*, issue #1075, April 2, 2009. Also online at: <http://www.informationclearinghouse.info/article22276.htm>.

James Petras, "Latin America: Perspectives for Socialism in a time of a World Capitalist Recession/Depression," online at: <http://petras.lahaine.org/articulo.php?p=1772&more=1&c=1>.

More Generally
Wallerstein, Immanuel, *Historical Capitalism*.
Hudson, Michael, *Super Imperialism*.
Chossudovsky, Michel, *The Globalization of Poverty*.
Henwood, Doug, *Wall Street*.
Ingham, Geoffrey, *The Nature of Money*.
Kindleberger, Charles, *Manias, Panics, and Crashes*.
Hutchinson, Frances (and others), *The Politics of Money*.
McNally, David, *Against the Market*.

6
May Day Talk

Text of a talk given at the May Day noon rally in the City Hall Plaza in Boston on Tuesday, May 1, 2012, in the rain.

C*apitalists have always been criminals.* They have been willing to exterminate entire peoples in order to keep the profits rolling in. May Day stems from a capitalist crime. In 1886, in Chicago, during a period of intense class struggle, they rounded up eight anarchists and accused them of something they didn't do. Four were hanged a year later after a fake trial. These executions sparked an international furor of protest. May First was thereafter celebrated as a workers day in honor of the Haymarket Martyrs.

So here it is 126 years later and the crimes of capitalists are continuing unabated, except that they have now reached earth killing levels. Global warming, which is being caused by capitalists, has the potential of killing all life on earth. This is the mother of all crimes. But even their lesser crimes are now global in scope and destructiveness.

Thus it is more urgent than ever that we defeat capitalists. Fortunately, we are in a window of opportunity. The keenest scholars of capitalism and its history are agreed that we are entering a period of chaos during which no one nation will be hegemonic. This gives us an opening to establish a world full of democratic, autonomous commu-

Chapter 6

nities, free of capitalism, states, wage-slavery, hierarchy, markets, and money, a world without borders or war, based on peace and justice.

How to do it? That is the question, and always has been. We have tried many things. We must keep trying. We must be creative and keep inventing new tactics and strategies. One thing is for sure: we can never defeat them militarily. But this is not a plea for nonviolence. In fact, we must expunge that false debate from our thinking once and for all. Rather, it is a claim that we can only defeat capitalists by organizing ourselves socially in ways superior to theirs.

Why don't we pick up and run with two concepts from the recent Occupy Wall Street, and try to extend them? Occupations and Assemblies. Both practices have always been part of revolutionary movements. For example: during the Spanish Revolution factories and farms were occupied in key towns and provinces; during the French Revolution workers in Paris set up 48 assemblies, one for each section of the city. More recently, beginning in Chiapas in 1994, assemblies have been popping up everywhere, in Algeria, Argentina, Bolivia, Oaxaca, Greece, and just last year in Egypt, Spain, and finally in New York City.

If we could extend these assemblies to expanded households of 200 or more people, to neighborhoods, and to workplaces, we would begin to organize ourselves socially in such a way as to be able to defeat capitalists.

There is much merit in the recent slogan: "Occupy Everything." What does this mean? It means that we counter the capitalist drive to "privatize" everything, that is, to put everything under the control of corporations, with our own drive to place everything back into the commons, the public domain, into common ownership.

Traditionally, most anti-capitalists have believed that we could get rid of capitalism by capturing the state, either through an armed revolution or by winning elections. That has proved not to be the case.

This leaves us with the two anarchist strategies: anarcho-syndicalism and anarcho-communism. Certainly, as already indicated, taking over our workplaces, both profit and non-profit, will be a necessary part of defeating capitalists. And certainly, trying to create sustainable democratic communities is essential also. But we need something more. I'm not sure we any longer have the time to build a new society within the shell of the old, although we must keep struggling along that path. Our problem now is not how to defeat capitalists, but how to defeat capitalists quickly. We all need to be thinking hard about how to do this.

First, we need to attack the very idea of the state. Capitalists and their states are inseparable. We cannot get rid of capitalists without also getting rid of the state. So we should organize a massive and vigorous campaign to discredit the state, especially in its popular form of representative government, and to foster instead the idea of direct democracy, through popular assemblies. Then we should add to this a drive to build a strong global movement to stop paying taxes. Governments cannot exist without taxes.

Second, we need to focus on the big players, those who actually control the world, mostly through their control of money. This is what was so exciting about Occupy Wall Street. Finally, a group had put the spot light on the money-bags. A recent study by a research team in Switzerland identified these particular capitalists. They surveyed 43,060 transnational corporations, and the interconnections between them. They found that out of those, 1318 were the core, and that of those, only 147 controlled 40% of the world's economy. Many of them were banks.

We must break the control that these capitalists have over our lives. Just one tactic we might consider is to occupy all the stock exchanges of the world. Flood them with thousands of people and shut these casinos down. I'm sure we can think of other tactics too, like refusing to pay interest on loans, and even repudiating the very idea of debt.

But one thing we know: The oil companies must be stopped. Goldman-Sachs must be stopped. Monsanto must be stopped. The World Bank must be stopped. The CIA must be stopped. It is an absolute evil if there ever was one. The arms industry worldwide must be stopped. The Pentagon must be stopped. The corporate media must be stopped. All these institutions and many more like them must simply be overrun and dismantled.

So there is plenty to do for everyone. Let's get to it.

Thank You.

The text for this talk was posted shortly thereafter on the website www.bostonmayday.org. It was also published in the **Anarcho Syndicalist Review,** *#58, Summer, 2012.*

7
Loss of Anticapitalism

Review: *Audacious Democracy: Labor, Intellectuals, and the Social Reconstruction of America.* Edited by Steven Fraser and Joshua B. Freeman, Houghton Mifflin, 1997, 273 pages.

April 1998

Not one word about *destroying capitalism*! That is the most striking thing about this book. Not one word about abolishing wage-slavery. In fact the concept of wage-slavery is completely absent from this book. Instead, the assumption throughout is that working at a job for a wage is all there will ever be, the only issues being the conditions under which this work is done, its rewards, and the extent of state sponsored amelioration. Such is the depth to which the opposition in America has sunk, such is the thoroughness of the defeat of anti-capitalist forces, that radicals themselves now accept the permanence of the system of employers and employees, bosses and workers, buyers and sellers of labor-power. What a far cry from the blistering indictments of the boss system at the beginning of the century by Haywood, DeCleyre, Debs, and Goldman. You would have thought that at least Norman Birnbaum, Frances Fox Piven, Eric Foner, or Manning Marable, socialists all, could have spared a sentence or two

Chapter 7

for the ultimate goal. Not so however. Maybe they have lost sight of it.

The book contains 21 short essays (plus an introduction by the editors), presented at the "Teach-In with the Labor Movement" held at Columbia University in New York City in October, 1996. The conference brought together "leading American intellectuals and labor movement activists" (according to the jacket blurb). Seven of the 21 represent labor; six of these are with AFL-CIO, one with AFSCME. Of the intellectuals, twelve are professors and two are writers. One of the editors is a professor and the other is executive editor at Houghton Mifflin. Thus, the book is in no way representative of either labor activists or intellectuals, especially those not affiliated with large institutions.

A glance at the table of contents gives a hint about what we might be in for. There are articles on women and labor, Asian-Americans and labor, black leadership and labor, whiteness and labor, intellectuals and labor. We might surmise from this that identity politics has swamped the labor movement just like it has swamped the universities and the opposition movement in general, eradicating class analysis everywhere. But perhaps there is hope. There is an article on "Beyond Identity Politics." But we'll come back to this.

First let's take a look at the union bureaucrats. John Sweeney, in "America Needs a Raise," bemoans the passing of the boom days after World War II. "For employers back then, decent wages and benefits and high standards of corporate responsibility were seen as good business and good for business. And our leaders in government, business, and labor understood what President Kennedy said best: "A rising tide lifts all boats." Back then "We (my italics) were concerned with raising the standard of living for all Americans, not just accumulating wealth for the fortunate few." And things did improve – "...*a fair portion* (my italics) of the newly created wealth was distributed among the American *workforce* (my italics)." But the "Corporate irresponsibility became the strategy of choice in our new winner-take-all economy ...." "Even employers with proud histories of doing right by their workers joined the rush to speed up work, freeze wages, slash benefits, and eliminate pensions."

Sweeney documents the tremendous hit the American working class (he never uses this term however, saying instead "workforce", "working people", "American workers", or "employees") has taken over the last twenty-five years, and he wants to stop it. The way to stop it is to rebuild unions. Then you could make corporations stop exporting jobs, invest in America, provide training, and raise wages, and you could force the government to reform the tax laws, stop corporate welfare, and restore the safety net. "Our idea of a just society," says Sweeney, "is one in which *honest labor* (my italics) raises the standard of living for all, rather than creating wealth for just a few."

Of course there is zero analysis of why the boom ended, why the welfare state is being dismantled, or why factories are being moved overseas. The problem for Sweeney is "corporate irresponsibility," not the normal functioning of capitalism. His dream is to live permanently in the biggest boom, in the richest country, in the history of the capitalist system (which he completely accepts). This is the leader of organized labor in America speaking. His speech is so pathetic it's painful to write about it.

Robert Welsh details AFL-CIO's program for rebuilding unions. It sounds like a good initiative, provided your only objective is to "get a raise" for "workers."

Jose La Luz discusses new educational strategies to empower workers "to transform the existing power arrangements in order to improve the lives of working men and women." Nothing here about abolishing workers as workers and creating a society not based on, and entirely free from, the "employment" of "workers."

Mae Ngai outlines an informative short history of Asian workers in America, a history of exclusion primarily, and discrimination, linking this history to current debates

Chapter 7

about immigration. Once again though, the absence of anti-capitalism is obvious. "The real solutions," Ngai writes, "to workers' economic problems lie elsewhere [than in policing immigrants], in union representation, in living wages, in the enforcement of labor and environmental regulations, in higher workplace standards and in the retention of jobs in the United States." Isn't the real solution to workers' economic problems the abolition of capitalism – the destruction of the wage-slave system, the destruction of the labor market (the buying and selling of labor power), and the *end of exploitation*? How can there ever be a 'real solution' short of this?

Karen Nussbaum presents a standard discussion of the role and position of women in the labor market, and discusses recent organizing efforts. Her goal though is merely "... to restore balance in our world – between the rich and the rest, between work and family, between men and women...." Balance? Between the rich and the rest? Under capitalism? Give me a break.

Saddest of all though is Ron Blackwell's piece on "Globalization and the American Labor Movement." Blackwell complains that corporations "have escaped the reach of public authority and are pursuing their private objectives at the expense of the rest of society." Have they *ever* done anything else? He seems to think the problem "is not globalization itself but the irresponsible actions of corporations in regard to workers, unions and other social movements, and to governments ...." "Without countervailing power," he writes, "from other social forces [e.g., unions] or effective governmental regulations, there is no way to make private corporations fulfill their public responsibility ...." Well why not just *get rid* of private corporations? "Without effective regulations, corporations pursue profit with no regard for the wider social or environmental impact of their activities." "The challenge to the American labor movement is not to stop globalization but to restore a balance of power between workers and their employers and to make corporations accountable again to government and the people." Well golly gee! I must have been asleep to have missed this golden age of capitalism when corporations were accountable to the people. When was it? Even during the heydays of the post WWII boom, most countries of the world were being gutted and impoverished, toxic dumps were being laid down by the thousands, native and peasant cultures were being destroyed everywhere, whole nations were inflicted with artificially induced famines, whole huge sections of the working class were living on subsistence wages even in the rich countries, hundreds of millions of acres of land were being grabbed, the commodification of everything was proceeding at a furious pace, militarism was rampant, tens of thousands of species were being exterminated, rain forests obliterated, oceans polluted. When have capitalists ever behaved responsibly? Tell me that.

This essay is so preposterously naive, so thoroughly unaware of the fierceness with which capitalists defend, on a daily basis, their mechanisms of theft, so completely ignorant of the structures of capitalist rule through five hundred years of murder and plunder, that it is a shame the piece was ever printed.

Now let's take a look at the academics. First Todd Gitlin's "Beyond Identity Politics." Any hope we might have had that Gitlin would return to class analysis is quickly dashed. Gitlin likes identity politics; he just thinks it has reached its limits of effectiveness. Far from seeing it as having helped eradicate class analysis from the American left, he thinks it has accomplished a lot. That he sees "workers" as just another identity betrays his deep embeddedness in identity politics. He thinks it's time to add this identity, that of worker, to the others: women, blacks, gays and lesbians, Native Americans, Latinos, and so forth. This identity, of worker, gives us a new "commonality" he says, and will help us overcome "poverty" and "inequality."

But of course "worker" is *not* an identity category. It

Chapter 7

does not refer to a personal characteristic like gender or race, nor to a cultural characteristic like language or ethnicity. It is an analytical concept used by radical theorists to dissect capitalism. It is inextricably linked with capital – labor and capital – as the two poles of the profit system, "worker" being a name for one location in this system. It is a *relationship*, not an identity. And it is a relationship of subordination and exploitation, whether workers are aware of this or not. But it is only rarely that workers *have* been conscious of themselves as workers, let alone as wage-slaves. This consciousness was more widespread in the nineteenth century. It can be argued that this was because capital then had not yet fully colonized the consciousness of the working class. Workers then were still in possession of cultures predating capitalism, and still retained some non-commodified relations. Be that as it may, workers have long since stopped thinking of themselves as workers. It is questionable whether this consciousness can ever be revived, or whether it is desirable to even try. Capital itself, as part of its ideological defense, has destroyed this consciousness. Also, however, I believe that workers themselves have sloughed it off. Who wants to think of themselves as just a worker, a wage-earner? We are more. We are human beings, or at least citizens. Working at a job is something we have to do to survive, but it is not us. We have lives of our own to lead, and many interests outside work. So this can be turned to advantage in the anti-capitalist struggle. The original goal after all was to abolish workers as workers. So we have sloughed off the label, but we are still trapped in the relationship, a relation of abuse and slavery. It is this bondage that has to be sloughed off now. And it can be.

But Gitlin says none of this. His goals are merely "shorter work weeks, work-sharing, democratic controls over corporate policies [sic], health care, worker protection, [and] a reversal of the thrust toward inequality." Gitlin is a New Leftist who never made it to a class analysis and an understanding of capitalism, but remained encased in the old liberal, pluralist theory of democracy, which he then, along with thousands of others, imported into the radical movement and renamed identity politics.

The only sustained discussion of class in the book is in Lillian Rubin's "Family Values and the Invisible Working Class." This essay is a plea for keeping the category of "working class" and not lumping everyone in the middle class. But once again the pernicious influence of mainstream social science is quite evident. For Rubin, class is a matter of income or occupation level, not a question of your relation to the accumulators of capital, that is, of whether or not you have to sell your labor-power to live. So although she believes that there is still a working class (contrary to popular belief), she also believes that most Americans are in the middle class. Actually, income has nothing to do with class. That is, it is the source of income that determines class, not the amount. Workers who sell their labor-power for $100,000 a year are still in the working class. They can only escape the working class if they use some of that money to buy real estate, stocks and bonds, or profit-making enterprises, and thus begin to live off rent, interest, dividends, and profits, rather than wages or salary. But if they spend it all on houses, cars, boats, vacations, clothes, and entertainment, they remain workers, although rich ones. Many thousands of middle level managers have learned this all too painfully in recent years as they have been fired from their good jobs, and, unable to find another buyer of their labor at a similar price, have rapidly lost everything, ending up on the unemployment line or on welfare. They learned the hard way that they are workers who, in order to survive, have only their labor to sell.

The closest anyone comes in this book to rejecting capitalism is Norman Birnbaum, in the following sentence: "The subordination of the market by the nation and the extension of citizenship to the workplace remain the unful-

Chapter 7

filled tasks of American democracy." This is a rejection of capitalism only for those who realize: (1) that the "subordination of the market" implies the destruction of capitalism, since that is precisely what capitalism is – the domination of the market and commodified relations over all realms of life; and (2) that democratic citizenship in the workplace is incompatible with capitalism since capitalism by definition is precisely the monopolization of the means of production by the accumulators of capital. But how many are going to, or can, read between the lines like this? And the statement is marred in other ways, by his reliance on "the nation," for example, as if creating the nation-state system wasn't how capitalists managed to set up the market in the first place, and send its tentacles out over the entire world. Also, for a radical scholar to be still speaking of "American democracy" is very disheartening.

All the authors included here hope for the revival of the labor movement. What they seem to have forgotten is that for over a hundred years, from the 1830s until World War II, labor struggles were rooted in an anti-capitalist working class culture. Of course, there were reformist unions, what we now call business unions, from the very beginning, but they were surrounded by communists, anarchists, socialists, and anarcho-syndicalists. All this anti-capitalism has been swept away. At some point the term 'labor movement' was substituted as a euphemism for communism and anarchism by unionists who wanted to disassociate themselves from their more radical comrades, choosing instead to agitate only for small gains within capitalism, rather than for its overthrow. Can the "labor movement" be revived in the absence of anti-capitalist sentiments? Will workers fight again just for a raise? I have my doubts. I think we have passed through the welfare state phase, never to see it again. Workers, and their associations, will have to become revolutionary again, that is anti-capitalist, before they can hope to organize anew and fight effectively. A raise is not enough. *Freedom*, from drudgery and bondage, will have to be desired.

There are moments of relief in the book. Piven (and also Fletcher, the best of the labor pieces) offers a detailed and informative analysis of how recent legislative changes in Social Security, Medicaid, food stamps, welfare (especially AFDC), etcetera, are forcing millions of people back onto the labor market, thus expanding the "reserve army of labor" and weakening the power of labor vis-a-vis capital. She focuses especially on "workfare" and shows how this program is undermining unions and undercutting organized labor. Fonder and Birnbaum both present very interesting thumbnail sketches of the history of intellectuals and labor. Rorty reminds us that workers' struggles have not all been sunshine and flowers but usually have been rather brutal and bloody. Marable analyzes the differing strategies black leaders have adopted, stressing alternatively race or class, in trying to improve the conditions of African-Americans.

So there you have it. In short, there is not one audacious thought in this whole book.

If ever there was an urgent need for the infusion of anarchist ideas into the American left it is now. The total bankruptcy of statist strategies, whether Leninist or Social Democratic, could not be more glaringly apparent. Fortunately, there are revolutionary currents not noticed by the essayists in this book. The burgeoning anarchist movement in many countries, the autonomia in Italy and elsewhere, native and peasant uprisings like the Zapatistas in Mexico, the rediscovery of anti-Bolshevik communism, the continued development of autonomous, non-sectarian marxism, the still active anarcho-syndicalist organizations, mass anti-statist communists parties in India, localist movements in Africa, the regionalism of radical environmentalists, plus revolutionary theorists like Ellen Meiksins Wood, Colin Ward, Cornelius Castoriadis, Antonio Negri, David McNally, Carole Pateman, Immanuel Wallerstein, Silvia Federici, Harry Cleaver, David Noble, Selma James

– all these point the way to the renewal of the anti-capitalist war and the liberation of humanity from the bondage of wage-slavery.

This review was published in the **Libertarian Labor Review,** *#23, Summer 1998.*

8

A Great History of Capitalism

Review: Giovanni Arrighi, *The Long Twentieth Century: Money, Power, and the Origins of Our Times.* London: Verso, 1994, 2nd edition with an added 15-page Postscript, 2010, 416 pages.

May 2012

This is a truly remarkable book, the best I've read in years, perhaps ever. If you want to understand capitalism, this is the book to read. But it is mis-titled. The book actually covers the entire history of capitalism from its very beginnings in Italy in the 14th century, not just the long 20th century.

Capitalism expanded not in a smooth linear fashion but in a staggered series of steps or jumps, each of which made it more powerful. There were four such leaps, each made by a different capitalist ruling class, or the four great hegemons of capitalism, centered in Genoa, Amsterdam, London, and New York. That's what this book is about, these four great expansions in the accumulation of capital. What patterns were common to all? What was distinctive about each? How were the transitions from one to another accomplished?

Each of the hegemons rose to supremacy and then

Chapter 8

declined over a "long century." The first, the long fifteenth-sixteenth century, centered in Genoa, ran from about 1340 to 1630, or 290 years. The second, the long seventeenth century, centered in Amsterdam, ran from about 1560 to 1780, or 220 years. The third, the long nineteenth century, centered in London, ran from about 1740 to 1930, or 190 years. The fourth, the long twentieth century, centered in New York, runs from about 1870 to the present, or about 140 years. But since the New York hegemonic cycle is already well into its terminal crisis, this will be the shortest life-span of a capitalist hegemon so far. Each cycle of capital accumulation has gotten shorter, even though each was simultaneously more widespread and powerful.

The main feature shared by all four cycles of capital accumulation is that each cycle had two phases. The first phase, starting off the cycle, was a vigorous expansion of commodity production and trade. The rate of profit from this eventually begins to fail. The second phase therefore was a shift of emphasis onto finance and speculation. The point at which the owners of capital started withdrawing from material production and moving into finance, as the best way to continue making profit, Arrighi calls the signal crisis of the cycle, signaling as it does the beginning of the decline of a hegemon.

As should be obvious to all, for the past several decades, we have been in the financial speculation phase of the fourth great systemic cycle of capital accumulation. This really helps clarify what is happening to us, and puts current events into a much needed longer historical framework.

So this is what the book is about in broadest outline. But what makes it riveting is the rich historical detail recounted by the author. Arrighi himself is writing on quite an abstract level, but his story is infused throughout with concrete, empirical, historical data. A vast amount of outstanding scholarly research into capitalism has been accumulated over the past half century. That any one person could survey, absorb, and synthesize this body of knowledge and mold it into a coherent history is almost beyond belief. But he has done it – an astonishing accomplishment.

Capitalism originated in the city-states of northern Italy. There had been a great expansion of production and trade in the late thirteenth and early fourteenth centuries. But this was not capitalist. (All this is according to Arrighi, of course.) There were many centers of this trade, with none being hegemonic. Within the city-states, there was no distinction between business and government – these functions were completely intertwined. In fact, one of the long term trends which Arrighi discovers is the 500-year transition from capital being embedded in the state, as in the early Italian city-states like Venice, to the state being embedded in capital, as in the contemporary United States.

What happened is that the expansion of the trade networks of these city-states reached its limits, and profits began to fall. So the surplus capital that had been accumulated was shifted over to building up the state, waging war, and financial speculation (except for Genoa). This is how the second phase of the cycle always begins, with the over accumulation of capital. (And my God! Isn't this still agonizingly true today: the huge accumulation of surplus capital which is sloshing around the world, with nowhere profitable to go in the real economy, is pouring into financial speculation, wars and weapons, and to building up police states.)

Part of the Italian surplus capital was used to finance northern European governments and their wars. Florence became a major creditor. And this also was the beginning of another feature of capitalism – the control of public finances by private creditors (just as Wall Street now controls the U.S. Treasury, and the "market" – private owners of surplus capital – is calling the tunes all across Europe). This first financialization that took place in northern Italian city-states was thus directly antecedent to the beginning of the first true systemic cycle of capital accumulation, carried out by the capitalist ruling class in Genoa.

Genoa eventually won the city-state wars (Venice, Milan, Florence, and Genoa being the major competitors). Instead of wars and government, Genoa poured its surplus capital into developing new trade networks. It made a deal with "Spain." Spain handled the wars; Genoa managed the trade. This arrangement helped Genoa to become the first great hegemon of capitalism.

Until it was overtaken by Amsterdam. I won't try to summarize that transition, or the subsequent transitions to London, and then to New York, or how each new hegemon managed to expand the capitalist system. But I hope this brief sketch of the beginning of the story is tantalizing enough to whet your appetite so that you will read the book.

Another great thing about the book is that Arrighi tries to answer the question as to what comes next. Will a new capitalist hegemon emerge to replace the United States? Will there be a fifth systemic cycle of capital accumulation? He published a book in 1999, *Chaos and Governance in the Modern World System* (with Beverly Silver and others) which deals with these issues, as does his last book, *Adam Smith in Beijing* (Verso, 2007, 418 pages). Arrighi explores the following three possible outcomes to our present historical juncture:

(1) The establishment of the first true world empire by the United States. This would be the end of capitalism because capitalism is based on competing capitalist ruling classes though their corporations and states. A world empire would appropriate surplus wealth through sheer political and military tyranny, as in the empires of old. Although this still could conceivably happen, Arrighi doesn't think that it will.

(2) The emergence of China as a new hegemon. For a variety of reasons, however, Arrighi pretty much dismisses the idea that China could become a fifth hegemon within

capitalism and launch a new phase of capital accumulation. If China becomes dominant it would most likely revert to its historical tradition and establish a non-capitalist market system. This would also signal the end of capitalism. I'm unfamiliar with this concept and don't really understand it. I've started reading *Adam Smith in Beijing*. Perhaps I will get its meaning by the time I finish. I get the impression though that he doesn't think this is all that likely either.

(3) That leaves, as the third possibility, a long period of chaos in the world social order, which I think Arrighi believes is the most likely outcome of present trends. But what happens next? What comes out of this period of chaos?

My one disappointment in the book, although one shouldn't be disappointed about something one couldn't really expect from a scholar writing in the Marxist tradition, is that it doesn't even enter its author's mind that this coming period of chaos might be an opening, an opportunity, to establish anarchy, that is, a world full of democratic, autonomous communities, free of capitalism, states, wage-slavery, hierarchy, markets, and money, a world without borders or war, based on peace and justice, a world social order, finally, built on equality, without ruling classes.

This review was published in the **Anarcho Syndicalist Review**, *#58, Summer 2012.*

9

A Leninist Looks at Venezuela

Review: Michael A. Lebowitz, *The Socialist Alternative: Real Human Development*. New York: Monthly Review Press, 2010, 191 pages.

February 2011

*I*t has been a while since I read a book which I disliked as much as this one. More than dislike: disbelief, bafflement, exasperation, anger. The first thing to puzzle out is who on earth could Michael Lebowitz possibly be writing for? How many contemporary anti-capitalist revolutionaries are going to be impressed by favorable quotations from Comrade Lenin? Lenin destroyed one of the greatest peasant and worker revolutions in history. He systematically dismantled the Workers Councils (Soviets) and betrayed and smashed the peasants' drive for autonomy. He established a secret police (Cheka) and suppressed all opposition to his policies, including that of the Mensheviks, left socialists, and anarchists. He sent the Red Army against the anarcho-communist revolution in the Ukraine. He crushed the Kronstadt Revolt, the last gasp of the revolution in Russia. The Bolsheviks were vigorously repudiated almost immediately by anarchists, left libertarians, and council communists. Lenin was thoroughly demolished as a revolutionary thinker by Anton Pannekoek (among many others) in his little masterpiece, *Lenin as Philosopher* (1937). Twenty years ago, Lenin's creation, the USSR, disintegrated and simply vanished from the world, a massive historical failure. Who gives a damn anymore about what Lenin thought? The fact that Lebowitz thinks he can score points by quoting Lenin with approval shows what an extremely restricted intellectual and political world it is that he inhabits.

But these few Lenin quotes were just tossed-off side remarks (one critical citation, it's true). What is Lebowitz's primary methodology? Karl Marx. Everything derives from Marx, if Lebowitz is to be believed. There is hardly a paragraph in the book where he doesn't quote or cite Marx. He has set himself the task of reinventing socialism for the twenty-first century. He just assumes that the way to go about this is to go back to Marx for theoretical guidance, both as to the goal and the strategy for revolution.

Go back to the "real" Marx, that is. My god! As if we needed another exegesis of the "real" Marx, an endeavor that began with Marx himself who declared in 1883 "I am not a Marxist." Thousands of others have gotten in on this fun during the 128 years since then. Already in the 1890s Antonio Labriola in Italy put forth a Hegelian Marxism that was much at odds with the positivist Marxism of the Social Democrats in Germany. But the main effort to recover the "real" Marx began in earnest in the 1920s with the Hungarian philosopher Georg Lukacs and with the Left Communists in Germany and Holland (Karl Korsch, Anton Pannekoek, Herman Gorter), to be followed thereafter by the Frankfurt School, French Hegelian Marxism, the *Socialism or Barbarism* group, the Situationists, Italian autonomous Marxism, and, more recently, Open Marxism (to mention just a few currents within Marxism itself, leaving aside left libertarians and anarchists).

Lebowitz seems oblivious to all this. He cites Oscar Lange and Eugeny Preobrazhensky, as if these debates from the 1930s are the most relevant ones for today's concerns. The main contemporary theorist he turns to for help, citing him several times, is Istvan Meszaros, author of *Beyond Capital*. As is apparent from this brief survey, Lebowitz's methodology, and the skewed scholarship it is based on, is seriously flawed.

But anyway, what were the results? What did he come up with? Lebowitz calls his reinvented socialism "The Socialist Triangle," the three pillars of which are: (1) the assertion that all wealth is socially created; (2) the demand for common ownership of the means of production; and (3) the goal of full development of human potential, both individually and socially. Is it just me or is this actually old hat? Sure sounds like it to me. This is not reinvention; it is regurgitation. These principles have been part of the anticapitalist movement from the beginning. Half the book is devoted to spelling out these principles. It is an adequate, if not very inspired, description of a society liberated from the yoke of capitalism.

The trouble begins in the second half, which is devoted to strategy: How do we get there? Believe it or not, Lebowitz tries to refurbish and re-launch the by-now thoroughly discredited two-stage strategy for getting to communism: first capture the state and then use the state to get to communism. Except that he spurns use of the word communism because it is too soiled, preferring instead to name the final end of the revolution "socialism."

How does he go about such an anachronistic exercise? By my measure, through a sleight-of-hand. He pulls a definitional fast one. He simply redefines as a state something that is not a state. So he ends up with two kinds of state, the old one and the new one. The new one is democratic, participatory, and decentralized. It is based on workers councils and neighborhood assemblies. It is a self-governing, cooperative society.

Well, this is not a state. It is anarchy. How is it that Lebowitz does not recognize this? I would guess that it is

Chapter 9

because he probably suffers from the typical Marxist disease of hating anarchism, and so has not studied its literature or history, and is therefore probably ignorant and unaware of it.[1] Yet workers self-management is a theme of his book, as are neighborhood assemblies. Both these practices come from the anarchist tradition, not the Marxist. There is a vast literature about workers self-management created by anarcho-syndicalists, council communists, and guild socialists. There is a similarly vast literature about community self-government created by anarcho-communists.

Lebowitz appropriates these ideas (without crediting anarchism) but distorts them by forcing them into a Marxist, social democratic framework. The councils will only "take increasing control over matters directly affecting them," he says. He sees "these councils as the elemental cells of the new socialist state" (p.139). How weird is this!

Lebowitz's strategy is to use the old state to bring this new "state" into existence. What about the near century-long failure of numerous social democratic governments in Europe and elsewhere to do this very thing? What does he have to say about that? He says it was due to "the process of yielding to and thereby enforcing the logic of capital." (p.133)

I'm sorry, but this just doesn't cut it. The strategy of

---

[1] There is a curious sentence on page 132. "Marx understood that you cannot change the world without taking power." This can't be a coincidence, I thought. It's got to be an allusion to John Holloway's book, *Change the World Without Taking Power*. My suspicion was confirmed when I came across a footnote on page 183 (#18) where Lebowitz writes: "One can only laugh at those who think that this is possible without taking the power of the state away from capitalists." He laughs because for him Marx is God and Marx admonished workers to seize political power (see p.112). Holloway's book provoked a storm of protest from orthodox Marxists, so Lebowitz could hardly have missed it. He can laugh all he wants, but it is the laughter of a deluded man. Holloway's book is brilliant, cutting edge, important. It resonates with the living anti-capitalist movement. Whereas Lebowitz's book is antiquated, and speaks only to the dead past, to the moribund remnants of sectarian Marxism-Leninism.

social democracy failed not because the socialists who came to power weren't smart enough, dedicated enough, or revolutionary enough. It failed because the nation-state system is an integral part of capitalism and always has been. That is one of the ways capitalist ruling classes are organized, through their states. They are completely enmeshed in and depend on their states to define and defend property rights, destroy the commons, enforce wage-slavery, adjudicate disputes between corporations, maintain the market, build infrastructure, operate the international financial system, protect trade, stop theft, expand the enclosures, deploy armed forces to seize lands and resources, assist in the commodification of everything, suppress all opposition to profit-taking, block the emergence of real democracy (direct democracy), and a host of other things. They are not going to allow their states to be turned against them.

Yet Lebowitz thinks otherwise, that this state, which is a creation of capitalists, and is owned and controlled by them, can be captured by "workers" and turned against capitalists. He seems to think that the state is something separate from capitalism, rather than integral part of it. He has a long list of things this worker-captured state is going to do to undermine capitalism and to bring into being the new "state" (i.e., the self-governing society), things like taxing surplus value, forcing businesses to open their books to workers, transforming the working day, setting aside time on the job for workers to study management, and so forth (p.133 ff). Fat chance, I'd say.

How is it, by the way, that "workers" are able to get control of this "old" state? Throughout most of the book Lebowitz takes it as a given that they have done so. The discussion is about what to do then? But in the last chapter Lebowitz finally gives the game away, in a section called "Finally, The Party." A party, it seems (or a "political instrument," his preferred jargon), will after all be necessary to provide leadership and vision, and to build unity, because a popular movement "by itself ... cannot develop

Chapter 9

a concept of the whole – that is, it cannot transcend localism" (p.162). Uh oh! We've heard this before, haven't we?[2] He is at pains to persuade us that this will be a party of a new type, but I wasn't persuaded at all. How will this new party capture the state? He doesn't say, but given his general orientation, we can surmise that it won't be through armed struggle but by winning elections. So this puts us smack dab back into electoral politics: not a good bag to be in these days, when the era of representative government is rapidly drawing to a close.

Moreover, the era of the capitalist welfare state is also rapidly coming to a close. Forty years of neoliberal counter-revolution has dealt it a serious blow. Can it be revived? I doubt it. It seems clear that this phase of capitalism is done and gone, and it will not be coming back, except perhaps for brief periods in anomalous places. It was possible to begin with only because of massive labor movements which were rooted in communist, socialist, and anarchist working class cultures. But also, it was possible because capitalists were rolling in cash from one of the biggest boom periods in the history of capitalism. So they could afford a bit of welfare for the masses. But now the labor movements are gone, the radical cultures are gone, and the surplus profits are gone. So the welfare state is being rolled back even in Europe, where it was strongest.

Michael Lebowitz disagrees, however. He thinks that anti-capitalists can still capture the state and use it to improve the lot of workers, and even to start building a self-managed society from below, using state resources. Where in the world are all these beliefs coming from? Venezuela. Michael Lebowitz, an economics professor at Simon Fraser University in Vancouver, Canada, has served as a consultant to Hugo Chavez in Venezuela. *The Socialist Alternative* is sort of a rationalization, an intellectual justifica-

---

2 Vladimir Lenin, "...the working class, exclusively by its own effort, is able to develop only trade-union consciousness..." from *What is to be done?* [1902], *Collected Works of V.I. Lenin*, Volume IV, Book II, page 115, New York: International Publishers.

tion, for Chavez's programs. Chavez's government is fostering worker and community councils. It has also greatly improved the lives of average citizens with vigorous health and education programs. This is the basis for Lebowitz's rosy revival of social democracy.

The question is: What will come of it all? Is Venezuela just an anomaly, a throw back, or is it the wave of the future? Will Chavez's Bolivarian Revolution in Venezuela finally succeed in getting to true socialism, thereby breaking the century-long record of failure chalked up by social democratic regimes the world over? Is it possible to realistically look forward to the dismantling of the Venezuelan state? And its replacement by an association of autonomous, self-governing workplaces and neighborhoods?

There is a small group of anarchists in Venezuela which offers a rather different perspective on these questions than that of Lebowitz. They publish a periodical called *El Libertario*. We'll take a quick look at some of their work shortly. But first I want to lodge a few more complaints about Lebowitz's analysis.

First, following Marx's definition of communism as a free association of producers, Lebowitz speaks throughout the book only about "producers." Not free human beings, not citizens, not neighbors, but only producers. So he extends the identity of "worker," as defined by capitalists, into a general social analysis. We've got to stop doing this. One feature of a society without capitalists is that the distinction between work and not-work would be erased. Our life activities would become whole again, integrated. We need to start thinking this way now. Actually, capitalists themselves have given us a leg up on this because they have managed to turn the entire society into the means of production, into a social factory, to accumulate capital, so the distinction between production and everything else is no longer relevant anyway.

Second, Lebowitz has a strong tendency to write from the stance of a social engineer. He is constantly talking about "producing new humans" who are capable of self-government. His strategy proposals are designed, he insists, to "produce" the new socialist person. I found this extremely annoying. It is the baggage of Leninist vanguardism which Lebowitz is still loaded down with.

Third, when oh when will Marxists stop claiming the Paris Commune as their own (see p.115), when in fact they had almost nothing to do with it? If there was a dominant political tendency among the eighty-one delegates who made up the Paris Commune of 1871, it was anarchism, in the mutualist tradition of Pierre-Joseph Proudhon. Michael Bakunin wrote more insightfully about the Paris Commune than Marx did, but I doubt if Lebowitz is even aware of the essay, or of the other numerous anarchist accounts of the event.

Now back to the Venezuelan anarchists. They call themselves the Commission of Anarchist Relations. They have been publishing *El Libertario* (*The Libertarian*) since 1995, with 61 issues so far. The website for this periodical is <http://www.nodo50.org/ellibertario/>. I urge you to check it out. For those who don't read Spanish, there are more than sixty articles in English dating from 2005. There are also translations into French, Italian, Portuguese, and German. In general, they are critical of both the Hugo Chavez government and the US-backed opposition, as well as orthodox leftist parties. They call attention to the deals Chavez is making with transnational corporations, to the inherent contradiction between top-down, state-sponsored initiatives and genuine, autonomous self-government at the grassroots level, to the gap between the regime's rhetoric and the reality on the ground, and so forth. But I can't possibly give here even a sketch of their perspective on Chavez and the Bolivarian Revolution. I urge you to check it out for yourselves. The critiques are just a click away. I've provided a list of the more substantive articles in a footnote.[3]

In closing, I am bothered and saddened to trash a man's work like this. There are so few anti-capitalists left in the world. I'm sure Michael Lebowitz is a sincere revolutionary and wants to get out of capitalism and into a better world. It's just that the strategy he is pushing is a proven failure and has done and continues to do enormous damage to the anti-capitalist struggle. It is way past time it was buried and put to rest. We must, at long last, as anarchists have always insisted, simply bypass the state in our fight against capitalists and for a free society.

This review was published in the **Anarcho Syndicalist Review**, *#56, Spring 2011.*

---

3 "Introducing *El Libertario*," online at: <http://www.anarkismo.net/article/14405?print_page=true>.
"The Revolution Delayed: 10 years of Hugo Chavez's Rule," online at: <http://thecommune.co.uk/2009/02/09/the-revolution-delayed-10-years-of-hugo-chavezs-rule/>.
"An Antiautoritarian-anarchist perspective about Venezuela's situation," online at: <http://www.nodo50.org/ellibertario/english/venezuelasituation.pdf>.
Michael Staudenmaier, with Anne Carlson, "Of Chavistas and Anarquistas: Brief Sketch of a Visit to Venezuela," online at: <http://www.anarkismo.net/article/839?print_page=true>.
"Refuting the deaf: Chavism and anarchism in Venezuela," online at: <http://libcom.org/library/refuting-deaf-chavism-anarchism-venezuela>.

10
Peter Gelderloos Visits Boston

A Review of *Anarchy Works*.

July 2010

I suspect that over time Anarchy Works will come to be known as one of the finest books ever written about anarchy. Its author, Peter Gelderloos, had been thinking about writing a book about what anarchy would look like, but then, in a slight shift of focus, thought it better to write first about what anarchy *has* looked like. So he scoured the historical and anthropological literature for examples of lived anarchy. Then he mined these case studies (around ninety altogether he says) for insights about the whole range of theoretical and practical problems facing anarchists, everything from crime to exchange to work. This is a book that is thoroughly grounded in reality, in actually existing anarchy, both past and present. It can be put on the shelf alongside Colin Ward's 1973 classic, *Anarchy in Action*, which was also based on existing concrete social practices. As the title suggests, the book is an attempt (and a successful one) to refute the oft-voiced objection: Anarchy could never work.

Peter was on tour promoting this book. He came to Boston in late May, and then headed on up to Vermont, and then to Canada. He gave two talks, on May 25 and 26, both at the Encuentro Five space in Chinatown. In the first talk, which was attended by about thirty-five people, he presented various themes from the book. During the second evening, with about twenty present, he told the story of the squatter's movement in Barcelona. Lively discussion followed each presentation.

Peter Gelderloos was born in Morristown, New Jersey, but grew up variously in Tokyo, Seoul, and a suburb of Washington, D.C., ending up in Harrisonburg, Virginia, in the Shenandoah Valley. After high school he enrolled in James Madison University in Harrisonburg, but bolted after only three semesters for more engaging activities elsewhere, including a six month stint in the slammer for his 2001 arrest for protesting the School of the Americas at Fort Benning. In recent years, he has spent considerable time in Europe. From July 2006 to April 2007 he biked and hitchhiked from Berlin to Barcelona, via Russia, Ukraine, and Greece.[1] Just as he was about to leave Spain to return to the United States, he was arrested on April 23, 2007 on trumped up charges of public disorder. This involved him in a two-year legal battle, during which time he was obliged to stay in Spain. He was finally cleared of all charges in March 2009 and was free to leave the country.[2]

Gelderloos is most famously the author (notoriously in some circles) of *How Nonviolence Protects the State*, first published in 2005.[3] This is a blistering critique of the ideology of nonviolence, an ideology which is pushed relentlessly by the (very violent) ruling class and its corporate media, and adopted by large swaths of the opposition move-

---

[1] His travelogue of this trip, *To Get to the Other Side*, was published online in 2010 (222 pages) at: <http://togettotheotherside.org>.
[2] Links to accounts of this episode can be found in the Wikipedia article about him.
[3] The first edition in 2005 was self-published under an imprint Gelderloos created, Signalfire Press. The second edition was published in 2007 by South End Press in Cambridge, MA. (SEP has now moved to New York City.) This is a much revised and expanded version. It includes a new chapter, now the longest in the book, about anarchist revolutionary strategy.

ment. He exposes the conservative functions this ideology serves. But the book is not necessarily an explicit argument *for* violence, especially as a matter of principle. In fact, one of the main themes of the book is that the habit of claiming that our choice is between violence or nonviolence is a bad one. This is a false distinction which must be abandoned. Yet, the elimination of violence, even as traditionally defined, as a matter of principle, as demanded by pacifists, is also unacceptable. Moreover, standard definitions of what constitutes violence are especially skewed, as are comparisons of the relative weight and incidence of state violence versus revolutionary violence. His objective is to break the stranglehold that the ideology of nonviolence has over questions of strategy and to open up the debate, thus allowing consideration for a variety of tactics.

Peter has also written one of the better manuals on consensus decision making, which is quite popular in anarchist circles. It's called: *Consensus: A New Handbook for Grassroots Social, Political, and Environmental Groups*, published in 2006 by See Sharp Press. There is an archive of essays by Peter Gelderloos since 2003 on the web at *The Anarchist Library* (19 items so far).

Now back to *Anarchy Works*. After an Introduction in which the basic principles of anarchism are briefly described – autonomy and horizontality, mutual aid, voluntary association, direct action, revolution, and self-liberation – the book is organized into eight chapters, as follows: human nature, decisions, economy, environment, crime, revolution, neighboring societies, and the future. In each chapter a series of questions is asked, such as: Aren't people naturally competitive? Who will settle disputes? How will people get healthcare? Who will protect us without police? How could people organized horizontally possibly overcome the state? What will prevent constant warfare and feuding? Won't the state just reemerge over time? It would be pointless here to recap his answers to these questions, that is, to summarize the substance of the

Chapter 10

book. You will need to read it for yourself. Let me just say though that overall his answers are spot on.

One of the things that I find most attractive about the book is the author's clear and uncompromising insistence that the existing society must be deliberately and vigorously attacked in every way possible. We can't just let things ride. We can't remain passive. We need to go after our oppressors. In fact, the book might be seen as a catalog of all the various ways different peoples have invented, over the centuries, to resist their oppressors.

There is one novel idea in the book I'd like to call attention to, one I've heard only once or twice before, and quite recently at that. The still existing so-called archaic societies (what used to be called "primitive" peoples) sprinkled around the world, especially those living in hill country or on other marginalized land, may not after all be just remnants of ancient societies that have somehow escaped the influences of civilization. Some of them may be contemporary instances of people who have deliberately rejected and escaped from nearby states. Gelderloos pays particular attention to how these various peoples have organized themselves and to the tactics they have invented to avoid domination by their authoritarian neighbors.

This is a hard book to fault. But after careful scrutiny I find that I do have a few quibbles, a couple of which I'll mention here. First, this is a very positive book, but I'm wondering if it is maybe a bit too optimistic. Gelderloos may be making it seem like we are farther along than we are (which actually may be a valid balance to the usual exaggerated negativism, and in particular, to my own personal propensity for doom and gloom). Sure, you can weave these ninety some-odd cases into a coherent whole *in a book*, but are they coalescing like that in reality? I had the same feeling after reading Chris Carlsson's *Nowtopia*. That book described a number of contemporary initiatives, like urban gardening, permaculture, outlaw bicycling, and the internet commons. My questions were: Okay, these are all worthy projects, but will they ever converge or jell into a movement that can defeat capitalists? What would have to happen for them to do so? I have the same questions about *Anarchy Works*.

Second, throughout the book, Gelderloos treats capitalism and the state as separate entities. This happens in part of course because states existed long before capitalism appeared on the scene, so we get in the habit of thinking of them as separate things, especially in a book which makes a broad historical sweep, collecting cases from all ages. But for the past five hundred years, this conceptual separation is a mistake and hinders the anti-capitalist struggle. Capitalism does not refer just to an "economy," but to an entire social order. The international nation-state system is an integral part of capitalism (profit-takers + politicians = capitalism). So defeating capitalists *means* abolishing their states, without which the private ownership of the means of production would be impossible. Whatever.

It seemed that Peter enjoyed his visit to Boston. He likes to party and dance and stay up late. We threw a couple of good ones for him. Maybe he will come back some day. In the meantime, good luck with your current projects, Peter, and thanks for an outstanding and very stimulating book.

This review was published in **BAAM***, #35, July 2010, the newsletter of the Boston Anti-Authoritarian Movement.*

11
Sicko

A Review of Michael Moore's Film of 2007.

July 2007

It's nice of course to hear someone say that health care should not be for profit, and to show how the insurance companies, drug companies, and HMOs put their profit-taking ahead of human life. But otherwise the film's analysis of the health care crisis in the United States is seriously wrong. Moore never mentions the word capitalism, nor does he attack an entire social system based on profit-taking, of which the health care system is just one instance. Moore never attacks capitalism per se, not here, nor in his earlier films. In *Roger and Me*, for example, he was merely pushing for traditional union demands, a better deal for the working class, not attacking wage-slavery as such (i.e., capitalism).

As regards this film about poor health care in the United States, capitalism would seem to be eliminated as a cause by Moore's examination of the health care systems in Canada, England, and France, all of which are capitalist societies but which nevertheless have universal free health care. Here is where the film goes badly awry. Moore makes it seem as if the health care systems in those countries are because people there have a different social ethic – they

Chapter 11

take care of each other – whereas here it's everyone for themselves.

This is nonsense. That Canada, England, and France have free universal health care is the direct result of the powerful socialist labor movements that existed in those countries. But this is never mentioned in the film. One interviewee in Canada attributed their free health care to the efforts of one man. For England, Moore explains that its National Health Service was established right after World War II. It was one of the first things the English did to pull themselves together and rebuild after the ravages of Nazi Germany's attacks. There is not even a hint that a powerful socialist labor party had come to power at that time which did much more than establish a National Health Service. It also nationalized huge chunks of the economy, that being the conception of socialism that was dominant at that time (national ownership = socialism).

For France, Moore shows the protest marches that take place whenever the free health system is threatened. The protest demonstrations he showed were the recent ones, most assuredly, because free health care is increasingly under attack across Europe, as the neoliberal capitalist offense gathers steam there. Europe's welfare states, wrenched from the ruling class through decades of massive socialist and labor struggles, are starting to be dismantled, as anti-capitalist cultures have been weakened and even destroyed. Moore makes no attempt to explain how the French got free health care to begin with. For that, he would have had to explain that the French have had a strong left, one of the strongest in Europe, ever since the French Revolution, with massive communist, socialist, and labor movements and parties.

All this history is left out of Moore's film. Well, of course, if you can't even mention the word capitalism (I'm pretty sure it was not mouthed once by anyone in the film), let alone even acknowledge the massive opposition generated by this death machine, you perforce have to take an ahistorical approach. The Canadian, English, and French just happen to have free health care, as a given, perhaps because they are less selfish, more compassionate people.

Which leads us to Moore's recommendation for people in the USA: We must become more compassionate, like citizens in Canada, England, and France. The film strongly implies, of course, although it is never explicitly stated, that the insurance companies must be gotten completely out of the health care business (although he did make this very explicit in subsequent interviews on television). But this does not reach the level of a political strategy. Strategy remains on the level of changing our own morality, of remembering that we're all in this together, that we're one big family.

Socialism was eliminated as an explanation of anything (even in Cuba) early in the film by Moore's ridiculing of the fear of "socialized medicine." You would think this would have had the opposite effect, of establishing that socialized medicine is better. But it didn't. Socialism can't be better. So it is just left out. (Although Moore did point out that we have socialized fire departments, postal services, schools, and libraries, so why not health care – not mentioning of course that the postal service is already partially "privatized," and that libraries and schools are under threat of being so; I guess fire departments are safe for the time being; but garbage collecting has already been turned over to corporations in most cities; and water departments are being sold off.)

What happened is that the central drive of capitalists, to commodify everything in order to make a profit off it, putting profit ahead of life even, got checked in Canada, England, France, and Cuba. It didn't in the United States, which is the most thoroughly capitalist society in the world. In the absence of strong socialist and labor parties here, corporations simply took over the health care system and turned it into a source of profit. They are doing this all over the world with regard to everything – water systems, education, parks, roads, lights, heating, health care, schools, armies, and even the government itself – everything. This is the neoliberal capitalist offense to destroy everything public and commodify every last thing on earth, even the wind.

A rich moment in the film for me was the newsreel footage showing George Bush signing the Medicare "reform" bill. If ever a scene could illustrate the meaning of the phrase "laughing all the way to the bank," this is it. He was literally laughing, with glee, and with his usual smirk, but almost with a look of disbelief that they were pulling this scam off. Anyone who thinks that Bush is a dimwit who doesn't know what he is doing is nuts.

Health care for profit indeed shows in an especially blatant way the insanity, immorality, and criminality of putting profits before people. But this is not at all atypical in a capitalist economy. The oil industry is willing to destroy the earth in order to keep the profits rolling in. Actually, the earth doesn't even enter into their calculations. The massive, multi-billion dollar food processing industry has no regard at all for people's health, for whether their products are nutritious or not. The only thing that matters is whether they can be sold. For then the money rolls in. Capitalists as a class have never given a hoot for workplace safety, and have only dealt with the issue when forced to, no matter how many people are dying in their operations. Putting profits before people can almost serve as the very definition of capitalism.

Is Moore aware of all this? Well, he did hint, in vague terms, in his interview with Amy Goodman on Democracy Now!, that the basic underlying problem was that we needed to change our relation to capital. But this is not attacking the profit motive directly, and he avoided saying the word capitalism. Is he a closet socialist who is tailoring his message to what he thinks will fly? Whether he does it on purpose or not, it would surely be better to come straight out and lay down the historically accurate radical analysis. Of course, if he did that, the film probably wouldn't be opening in corporate owned movie complexes across the country. Doesn't that just show though how thoroughly radical analyses of our social problems has been excluded from public discourse? But is that a reason for not making them? Will these half-assed, watered-down assessments get us anywhere? I don't think so.

It reminds me a bit of what has happened to the environmental movement, as succinctly summarized recently by Jeffrey St. Clair and Joshua Frank:

> Big green groups are not helping the situation. Their hands are tied by both the large foundations that pay their rent and the Democratic Party to which they are attached at the hip. They long ago gave up on challenging the system. Most groups today are little more than direct mailing outfits who have embraced a sordid neoliberal approach to saving the natural world. The true causes of planetary destruction are never mentioned. Industrial capitalism is not the problem, individuals are. Not the government's inability to enforce its weak regulations. Not big oil companies, or coal fired plants. These neoliberal groups argue ordinary people are to blame for the impending environmental catastrophe, not those who profit from the Earth's destruction.[1]

At least Moore fingers insurance and drug companies, and HMOs. But he doesn't finger capitalism.

Nothing will change in the United States as regards health care. Capitalists are too solidly entrenched. The entire political apparatus is in their hands. They will nev-

---

[1] *Counterpunch*, June 29, 2007, "Toward a New Environmental Movement: Kick Out the Corporate Bastards"

er agree to eliminate this huge source of profit for their insurance, drug, and hospital corporations. Moore is just whistling in the wind.

12
A Sketch of an Anarchist Revolutionary Strategy

(Excerpted from my essay "Seeing the Inadequacies of the Strategy Proposals of the Anarchist Communist Federation (UK)").

February 1999

Some persons become convinced that they are oppressed. They study and ponder the situation to discover the sources of that oppression; who is doing it and how they are doing it. They also imagine a situation in which they would not be oppressed; what it would be like, and how it would differ from the way things are now.

Let's assume that they decide that the key thing, the essential factor, in their oppression is that they are not free and that they have no control over their lives or communities. That is, they realize that they are slaves, wage-slaves, being controlled and exploited for the profit of someone else, and therefore that it is very far from a democratic society they are living in. They decide that they would prefer having some control over their own lives and communities, and prefer not to slave away for someone else's benefit, or have some government somewhere making all the rules. They would prefer to get together with their neighbors to decide things in common, and similarly at

Chapter 12

home and at work, they would prefer to assemble together with their work mates and household mates to decide how to do things, what to do with the things they make, how to divide up the work, and so forth.

So this is what they start doing. They start assembling together to try to govern their own lives, at work, in their households, and in their neighborhoods. It turns out that the ruling class is not too happy about their meetings, and in fact gets very angry that they are meeting like this. So the ruling class tries to bust them up. Naturally, these persons take steps to defend themselves and to get the ruling class off their backs. They learn how to defend the social arrangements they have created. They invent social weapons to neutralize the military might of their oppressors.

They are also aware of course that friends and neighbors of theirs don't all agree that they are oppressed, or that they are slaves, or that the society is not democratic. So they argue with these friends and neighbors, trying to convince them of the validity of their perception of the situation.

In the meantime they go on trying to establish these new decision-making arrangements they have dreamed up. But disagreements emerge about how to proceed. Some have been frightened and intimidated by the attacks of the rulers. They want to back off a bit, and to settle for what they think is realistic, for what they think they can get. So they start pushing for this, and laying out their arguments. But the arguments don't fly too well. Everyone has been through this so many times before. They have watched as the world has slowly disintegrated, as the social situation has degenerated toward collapse, with the environment spinning toward irreversible life-threatening decay. They have seen again and again that compromises gain nothing, except defeat. And time is short. So for once the fainthearted lose out. Those who want to settle for less are out politicked by those who want it all.

They are aware however that they have to rally wider

A Sketch of an Anarchist Revolutionary Strategy

support, outside the neighborhood, in order to win. So they publicize what they have been doing. They try to inform as many people as possible about their struggles, dreams, defenses. They especially shout to the far ends of the earth all the details about every attack the ruling class makes against them. They take their case to the court of world public opinion, trying to gain the upper hand morally, in the hearts and minds of people everywhere.

They also begin to withdraw from and to stop participating in (as this becomes possible) all the hierarchical, ruling class institutions that they now see as onerous. They especially try hard to stop being wage-slaves and to embed themselves instead in cooperative communal labor. More and more workplaces become cooperatively owned and operated. Fewer and fewer of the necessities of life are being produced by wage-slaves.

They also increase their efforts to persuade more people locally that the course they have chosen is the road to freedom and greater happiness and well-being. They establish contacts with other neighborhoods and try to work out agreements with them regarding common interests and problems. They work out trade agreements.

Slowly, more and more people begin to perceive the situation in a new light, by seeing the examples before them and the direct action that others are taking to gain control over their communities and to set up new social arrangements. More and more wealth and power begins to be taken away from the ruling class and returned to the communities from which it had been stolen. The attacks of the ruling class become more intense and frantic, and this of course has the effect of clarifying the situation even more, although at a terrible price.

As more wealth and power become available, these neighborhoods, now rapidly becoming autonomous, cooperative, and democratic, can publicize their experiences even more, and begin to make a dent in the cultural hegemony so long held by the masters, and can promote more intensely the democratic, autonomous, self-governing, decentralized, communal (that is, anarchist) way of life. This way of life becomes a concrete reality in more and more neighborhoods, and then in millions and millions of neighborhoods, villages, and small towns throughout the world.

At long last, the institutions of the ruling class, all those weapons of oppression, all those corporations, governments, schools, churches, cinemas, newspapers, armies, hospitals, museums, universities, courts, malls, police stations, television networks, and law firms, are nothing but empty shells, with no power to hurt anyone. They are relegated to the dustbins of history, buried and forgotten, by the wondrous new world full of free communal peoples. New statues are erected to honor the martyrs. New holidays are chosen to celebrate the victories, commemorate key battles of the war, and highlight the achievements and dreams of free communities. People dance and sing and play and love. Ten hundred thousand traditions bloom. And a Jubilee begins, which lasts until the end of time.

13

The Consolidation of Fascism, American Style
(Comments on the 2004 Presidential Election)

November 2004

First of all, the election was rigged.
A few weeks back I read an article by Bev Harris (of Black Box Voting) about the vote tabulating centers. There are a dozen or so in each state. These are the places where each precinct sends its vote tally. The computers in these centers are programmed by private corporations, secretly, beyond public scrutiny, and are completely open to fraud and manipulation. This was a new direction for her research. Until then she had focused on the possibilities of fraud from using touch screen voting machines which do not print out a paper ballot. In this new article she said that it really didn't matter what kind of voting machines were used in the local precincts, because the vote tallies could be manipulated much more efficiently in the vote tabulating centers. I never saw any follow up to Bev Harris' story about the vote tabulating centers, before the election.

For the past four years however there have been scores of reports about the stolen election of 2000, about vote suppression techniques, about the insecurity of the touch screen voting machines, and about the many inadequacies of the US voting system in general. These essays were all over the Internet, and the issue was periodically reviewed by such independent media outlets as Democracy Now, Flashpoints Radio, and Free Speech Television. Nothing happened. Well, something did happen: Congress passed the Help America Vote Act, with majority support from both parties, which effectively turned the vote count over to private corporations, practically eliminated paper ballots, failed to enact any of the many ideas for improving elections (like instant run-off voting, a national day off on election day, standardized procedures, or extension of the voting period), and did little else to correct the many problems of the US voting system. In other words, Congress voted to corrupt the system further rather than fix it.

Now reports and analyses of the 2004 election are coming fast and furious (on the Internet that is, not from corporate media or elected politicians). Bev Harris, Lynn Landes, Greg Palast, Louis Posner, Rebecca Mercuri, and dozens more investigative reporters are digging into the many anomalies of this election, like widespread voter suppression, the discrepancies between exit polls and the official vote count, lost or destroyed ballots, uncounted provisional ballots, discarded absentee ballots, impossible numerical results, insufficient voting machines in poor and democratic precincts, and so forth. Two substantive reviews of this research are already available: Alan Waldman, "How the Grinch Stole the White House ... Again," (http://www.onlinejournal.com/evoting/112004Waldman/112004waldman.html), and Ian Reed, "Election Fraud for Dummies," (http://www.reedandwrite.com/Dummies.htm). A website has been established to follow these efforts (www.stolenelection2004.com). There are of course the two Black Box Voting websites (blackboxvoting.com, and blackboxvoting.org). An initial bibliography of relevant research has been compiled by Michael Keefer, "Evidence of Electoral Fraud in the 2004 U.S. Election," and is available at: (http://www.globalresearch.ca/articles/KEE411B.html).

Democrats.com posts almost daily updates on the situation in Ohio.

So, a campaign is rapidly gaining strength to challenge the election. Whether it will succeed or not is another question. Although the election is not officially decided until December 12, with the selection of the electoral college, for all intents and purposes the election was decided on election night. After that it becomes a question of reversing an election already decided. An Administration that can cover up 9/11, remain unscathed through enormous scandals like Enron, invade another country under false pretenses and get away with it, suppress the knowledge that its president was a deserter from his military service, and lie about every piece of legislation it has ever passed, is not likely to be bothered by challenges to a stolen election.

An election in which the votes are counted by private corporations is ipso facto illegitimate. The actual count is irrelevant. If vote counting can be turned over to corporations, anything can. If there is anything which absolutely must remain in public hands, in a democracy, it is vote counting. The fact that this most public of all things has been, already, 'privatized', shows just how far advanced into fascism we really are. It shows just how thoroughly the neoliberal counter-revolution (which seeks to destroy everything public) has succeeded. It happened with hardly a beep from anyone, except a few intrepid researchers. I find it hard to believe that this fait accompli can ever be reversed, short of a revolution. Of course I hope that I am wrong.

Thus American pseudo-democracy is no longer even pseudo, although it still retains the appearance of democracy, in that people still go to the polls and vote. That the rulers have been able to institute fascism, while making it still appear to be democracy, testifies to the genius of the neo-fascists. But let us not delude ourselves that we have ever had real democracy in America. Even if this vote had been fair it would not have been fair, because the entire set

Chapter 13

up is unfair. The majority has never been a governing power in the United States. The ruling class has been firmly in control ever since 1789.

Naturally, it would be fabulous if this election could be rolled back and reversed. This would mean that Americans are not yet willing to live under fascism, and are still able to do something about it. After all, recent FCC rulings were stopped with a massive protest movement. Nevertheless, corporate control of the media is not even close to being broken. Fascists have already gained power, and have consolidated it further with this election, but can they hang on to it? Challenges to the election will eventually end up in the courts or in Congress, where they will be defeated, since these are already packed. Wouldn't we have to break corporate control of Congress before we could break corporate control of the media or elections? And will Congress ever vote for campaign finance reform? Of course not. So wouldn't all this practically take a revolution to achieve, which is of course what we should be working on.

Anyway, this is how you steal an election. Get control of the vote count, and then tweak the results just enough so that recounts won't be called for. As an added precaution, get rid of paper ballots, so that even if a recount is demanded, it will be impossible to carry out. Then get a news blackout on challenges, and have the Congress and Administration act as if the challenges don't exist.

It's pretty clear, from the facts already available, that this election was outright stolen, certainly in Florida and Ohio, and probably in the other swing states as well, like New Mexico, Nevada, Colorado, and Iowa. In addition, the Bush vote was undoubtedly enhanced throughout the country by tampering with the vote tallies in the tabulating centers. This is one way to account for the three and a half million victory margin for Bush in the popular vote.

Second, millions of Americans are brainwashed.

Another way to account for the vote is to recognize that

millions of Americans are simply brainwashed. But all this means is that the propaganda system is incredibly effective. The extreme right has been working on spinning this cocoon, within which millions of people live, for forty years. They have think tanks and public relations firms working on it around the clock, year in and year out. The Republican Right set out forty years ago to build an infrastructure to influence public opinion. They succeeded. So this is another way to steal an election – get people to vote the way you want them to so that you don't even have to bother to change their votes fraudulently after they vote.

Third, millions of Americans actually are fascistic in outlook.

But the brainwashing thesis goes only so far. Even if they flipped the vote count by five or ten percent, enough to give Bush a comfortable margin of victory, that still leaves millions of people who voted for Bush. Most of these people are decent folk, I'm sure. But some are not so decent. I think we have to admit that a sizable number of these millions are in fact aware of what Bush has been doing and condone it. They want the borders sealed. They don't care about those Iraqi deaths. They *are* often intolerant and mean. Some are bigoted and full of hate. Many are willfully and grossly ignorant, and think they have a monopoly on morality. They *like* empire and capitalism. Many are crooks and bullies themselves. They *don't* prize liberty above all else. They *don't* value democracy, but believe in authority and discipline. They don't believe in 'freedom and justice for all,' but in 'family values.' They ridicule environmentalists, and scoff at attempts to save endangered species. They demonize liberals, considering them to be an enemy which has to be crushed, eliminated. They are in denial about global warming and peak oil. They like the death penalty. They are religious fanatics. They are militarists and national chauvinists. They hate queers. They hate hippies, single moms, blacks, foreigners, atheists, secular humanists. We ignore this dark stain on the American character at our peril.

Of course, these attitudes and behaviors could themselves still be the result of a sort of long-term conditioning (manipulation, brainwashing). What kind of social order gives birth to and nurtures such degraded humans? It is important to know. But in the short run, it hardly matters, because after so many decades, this becomes how people really are.

Fourth, the Christian Right Played a Central Role in the Fascist Victory.

Christian fundamentalists have been correctly called Christo-Fascists. There can be no doubt that they delivered the victory to Bush. All our demonstrations, internet websites, progressive periodicals, videos, books, and independent media, were nothing compared to the one hundred thousand or more Christian Fundamentalist Congregations. These people meet every week, in their churches, to listen to sermons. Many of them are in church several other times each week, for prayer meetings, scout meetings, social functions, and priesthood meetings. They don't have to get organized, they already are. And they voted.

Most Christian Fundamentalists live in a kind of cocoon, and so cannot perceive what happens outside it. They have their congregations, so they are surrounded with people who believe like they do. They have their own bookstores now, their own novels, videos, textbooks, children's books, radio stations, tv stations. They have Fox TV and Rush Limbaugh. They home school. It is a self-enclosed world, and a self-reinforcing belief system. They are impervious to outside influence and criticism. They live in a world unto themselves. They have all these little narratives they tell themselves, like a completely specious history of the Israel / Palestine conflict. They also make up grand narratives, like a history of Western Civilization they have written and which many of them use in home schooling, which is a pure fabrication and bears little resemblance to what actually happened. Forty years ago, Christian Fundamentalists saw themselves as living in the world but not of it. Now they want to own the world, and to change it to conform to their image of what it should be, which is a world of dogma and theocracy. They want to take us back to the Middle Ages, before the Renaissance and before the Enlightenment.

How did this strange alliance between fascists and fundamentalists come about? Here is what happened, as I now understand it. Not long after the revolts of the 1960s were crushed, the extreme right-wing of the Republican Party realized that it could never come to power without a mass base. And they could never get a mass base while operating openly as the party of big business. So they set out deliberately to woo the Christian Right. They decided to go to bat for the Christian Right's social agenda (even though they themselves couldn't care less about these issues, their only loyalty being to corporate power and profit-taking). In other words, they started supporting Christian Fundamentalists on school prayer, abortion, homosexuality, ending the separation of church and state, curbing immigration, supporting faith-based welfare, fighting drugs, and so forth, across several more emotionally charged issues dear to Fundamentalists. It was a small price for them to pay to gain a mass base of support for their party. This was only part of the Right's counter offensive of course, although it was a large part. In addition, the Right set up numerous think tanks, organized the Federalist Society, got into talk radio in a big way, published books and magazines, funded Republican groups and newspapers on the nation's campuses, and eventually, in the 1990s, even set up their own television station, Fox News.

As it happened, this tactic of theirs coincided with a change of orientation on the part of Christian Fundamentalists. Two or three decades ago, Fundamentalists decided that they were no longer content to simply enjoy the reli-

Chapter 13

gious freedom they had in this country to believe whatever they pleased. They decided to go political and to capture the government in order to establish a Christian Nation. They set up radio and tv stations, did massive organizing in the thousands of fundamentalist churches, got their people elected to all levels of government, and launched the culture war against liberals and secular humanists. It was a determined campaign.

Both campaigns were wildly successful, and culminated in the stolen election of 2000, and now, more ominously, in the stolen election of 2004. Basically, Fundamentalists made a 'pact with the devil', that is, with Republican Fascists. Because of this unholy alliance, our freedoms are gone, and we have all fallen into the grip of fascism.

One thing has always puzzled me about Christian Fundamentalists, namely, how they can blithely ignore what the United States is doing overseas. Here are people who claim to be moral and to care about others, yet they turn a blind eye to enormous suffering and death in other lands caused by their own government. Just a few months ago, the US government overthrew a democratically elected President in Haiti. The coup was planned, financed, supplied, and organized by the US. And now the puppet regime they installed is systematically *killing* the leaders and supporters of the popular movement there which has been fighting for democracy and resisting US domination of their country. Hundreds of lives are being lost in a sustained, ruthless slaughter. Do we hear an outcry from Christian Fundamentalists? No. I guess as long as they get school prayers back, and get homosexuality outlawed, and get abortion stopped, they don't care how many lives are lost in foreign lands. In this sense, and in spite of their claim that their movement is based on 'moral values,' Christian Fundamentalists must be judged to be highly immoral people.

I listened to a two-hour post-election wrap-up on Democracy Now on Wednesday. Only two of the dozen or so speakers, Leslie Cagan and Danny Schecter, referred, in an off-

The Consolidation of Fascism, American Style

handed almost parenthetical way, to the Christian Right. The majority of these progressive commentators live in the Northeast. They are seriously out of touch with the rest of the country. (There was some discussion of the Christian Right however the following day on Democracy Now.) In a discussion I had a few weeks ago an acquaintance claimed that the Christian Right was no longer much of a factor in national politics. I wonder if he has changed his mind now.

— — —

And so on Tuesday we witnessed fascists in America consolidating power, the culmination of the their forty year struggle, beginning at least with the assassination of John Kennedy in 1963, to seize the government. They now control the Presidency, the Congress, the Supreme Court, the Federal Courts, the Media, most Governorships, and most State Legislatures. There will be no going back now to a liberal democracy. The Neocons will be able to stay in power indefinitely. It's not only that they now have the ability to steal elections. They have locked up the system in other ways as well, as for example through the scientific gerrymandering of congressional districts.

Many argue that it is an exaggeration to say that the United States has already become a fascist country. They might agree that it is proto-fascist, or semi-fascist, but not yet the real thing. I think they are wrong. We now have a regime which truly hates democracy, and which deliberately set out to destroy it. It has all the main characteristics of fascism. It has a mobilized mass base. It flows out of an abandoned democracy (that is, a population that is willing to give up its democratic institutions out of fear, in exchange, they think, for security). It operates completely outside the law, both domestic and international. It is characterized by the tight merger of corporations with the government, a melding with religion, extreme nation-

Chapter 13

alism and militarism, glorified patriotism, fear mongering, assassinations, aggressive foreign wars, suppression of domestic dissent, the corruption of science, the torture and murder of prisoners, corruption and outright criminality at the highest levels of government, destruction of unions, a monolithic propaganda machine, vicious attacks on the left, and a host of other similarities with classical fascism.

We have to realize though that it is a new, American style, fascism. It is much more sophisticated, by many levels, than Hitler's or Mussolini's fascism. Its propaganda machine is incredibly more powerful than the Nazi's. Moreover, American fascists are not facing, as German and Italian fascists did, massive and powerful working class cultures and movements of socialism, communism, and anarchism. I doubt if we'll see a jack-booted fascism (although who can forget the pictures of demonstrators being thrown to the ground by police and held there by a boot on the neck). I wouldn't want to call it a 'friendly fascism' though as Bertram Gross did twenty years ago.

The fact is that they don't need to get violent, on a regular basis, like the Nazis did (at least with the majority of middle income white Americans; they are plenty violent towards African and Native Americans, and the poor). They can get what they want without this overt violence. Their system of control is that much better. They can plunder the national treasury at will, go to war, destroy unions, suppress dissent, eliminate opponents, increase exploitation, imprison millions, break every law on the books, at will, without killing anyone (hardly). They can do all this while appearing to be legitimate, as has been proved just now by this 2004 election they engineered.

When they do need to get violent, they don't hesitate, like in Iraq, or Haiti, or Columbia, or like with the (very probable) assassinations of Wellstone and Callahan (in keeping with their tradition of murdering prominent liberal leaders, like John and Robert Kennedy, Malcolm X, Mar-

The Consolidation of Fascism, American Style

tin Luther King Jr., and Walter Reuther), or like with the suppression of the Miami demonstrations against the Free Trade Agreement of the Americas. Democracy Now, Indymedia, Free Speech TV, and Infoshop.org can be tolerated because they are not serious threats to the ruling class. If they ever do become serious threats, they will be smashed. They may even be smashed during Bush's second term anyway, even though they pose no threat, just because it can be done. Who knows, maybe the fascists already do feel threatened, and now that they have solidified their power, will move aggressively to suppress dissent across the board. After all, historically, the first order of business for fascist regimes after gaining power has been to destroy their left opposition. In the US, the fascist structures of repression are now firmly in place, and have already been used on targeted populations.

The neocon fascists and the christo fascists, between them, have big plans for the United States. They intend to roll back the twentieth century. The neocons want to take the country back to the days of the Robber Barons and before, to the days of unfettered capitalism. They want to get rid of every last regulation which constrains business. They want to destroy everything public, so that all needs will have to be met through corporations, which will charge whatever they please. They want to reverse the New Deal, abolish all taxes on the rich and corporations, eliminate the income tax, and steal the Social Security fund by 'privatizing' it (and eventually abolish it altogether). They will use the government only to grease the military-industrial complex, bail out failed corporations, transfer wealth from the poor to the rich, fight imperialist wars, and suppress any opposition to these policies, while eliminating any role for government in helping ordinary people. They have no problem at all with 'big government', in spite of their claims, as long as it serves empire and capital, not the average joe and jane. The christo fascists want to reverse the sexual, gender, and feminist revolutions, and reestab-

Chapter 13

lish the patriarchal family. They hate feminists almost as much as they hate homosexuals. They seek to establish biblical law as the law of the land, and to set up a theocratic state (a Christian Nation).

— — —

In one election postmortem I read, the author, Michael Albert, recalled the election of 1972, in which the liberal candidate George McGovern lost in a landslide to Richard Nixon. McGovern carried only one state, Massachusetts. So Albert concluded that this 2004 election didn't mean that we have entered into some kind of fascism, because the same thing happened way back then, in an even more extreme way. I disagree. The situations are very different.

In 1972, the more liberal wing of the sixties New Left, those interested in electoral politics, had taken over the Democratic party and the Democratic Convention, and nominated an anti-war and anti-empire (a little bit) candidate. (I should clarify that McGovern was endorsed only by the liberal wing of the anti-war movement, not by New Left radicals and revolutionaries.) He was probably the most progressive candidate since Roosevelt. But he became the symbol, on the national electoral level, of the revolts of the sixties. The vast majority of Americans hated the radicals of the sixties. Their response to the end of the American Dream (which shattered irrevocably on November 22, 1963, with Kennedy's murder), was to turn their anger on the sixties revolutionaries. So they rejected McGovern, resoundingly, in a sort of spontaneous outrage.

I think my own personal experience in this was in fact typical. I lived in New York City throughout the sixties. My parents lived in Missouri. They were absolutely horrified by my behavior, and I don't think it was entirely because of our being badmouthed by the media (we had of course gotten bad press from the outset). They were genuinely appalled. I had turned against everything they believed in, or so they thought.

But the situation now is rather different. This right wing victory was carefully engineered, and was the culmination of a forty year drive to seize power. They used the opportunity they gained from the stolen election of 2000 to dig in, strengthen their institutions across the board, and pull off a real, decisive victory this time around, in the form of another spectacularly, and openly, stolen election. One ray of hope though is that they did after all still nevertheless have to steal the election. They don't yet have a majority in their camp, in spite of all their think tanks, PR firms, and mass media.

On second thought, there may after all be a similarity between the elections of 1972 and 2004. For what has happened these past few years? Well, protest movements have exploded everywhere, beginning in November 1999 in Seattle, and then moving on to Philadelphia, Los Angeles, Washington DC, Boston, Miami, Quebec City, Genoa. I suspect that when the tens of millions living in the Midwest, South, Great Plains, and Rocky Mountains, saw a million protesters marching through the streets of New York City at the Republican Convention, that's when they resolved that they would make damn sure to get out and vote for Bush. Nearly half of all Americans hate protesters, and anything that upsets the status quo. And they hate New York City, regarding it almost as an alien state, being as it is a liberal bastion.

At least with McGovern progressives had a candidate who embodied a few of the values and goals of the protest movements of the sixties. With Kerry, they had nothing. Nevertheless, the progressive movement was determined to vote for him, because of the extreme danger represented by the Bush neocon cabal. Conservative Americans understood this, understood that Kerry was the candidate of the protesters (and a Massachusetts liberal to boot). This was enough to motivate the millions in the heartland to get out the vote to defeat him, just like McGovern was defeated in 1972 (in what was surely one of the most humiliating defeats in US electoral history).

Of course, there are many other reasons for this current Democratic defeat, other than conservative revulsion at protesters, which was after all probably not the major factor. (Please note that I've said "defeat", and not that they "lost the election", which I don't believe they did.) The decisive factors were surely that the Republicans have built a mass base among Fundamentalists, have invented and gained acceptance of a whole new ideology, have instituted fascism which gives them a lot more control, have prosecuted the 'culture wars' relentlessly, have learned to speak a totally Orwellian language, and have defined their opposition as an 'enemy' to be eliminated, not just bested at the polls. There is the additional fact that Democrats have been for a long time now merely Republican-lite, and offer nothing to the average citizen.

I was distressed almost as much by progressive commentary after the election as by the election itself. Howard Zinn for example was a participant in the radio program I mentioned above, on postmortems on the election. He said we should not lose hope, but work harder to build a movement for change to try to move the Democratic Party to the left, or perhaps start a third party for progressives. This same sentiment was expressed by every progressive commentator I heard or read after the election. These people never learn.

Several mass movements have been built in American history, all aimed however only at changing laws. The abolition movement sought to get rid of chattel slavery, by law. The suffrage movement sought to give women the vote, by law. The civil rights movement sought to secure basic constitutional rights for African-Americans, by law. The environmental movement sought to protect the environment and save endangered species, by law. These kinds of movement are no longer sufficient. (Actually, they never were.)

We need to build a movement, for sure, but for what? To radicalize the Democratic Party? No! To build a third Progressive Party? No! To get populists elected to Congress, to get proportional representation, to get instant runoff voting, to get a multiparty system, to get money out of elections. No, No, No, No, and No! We definitely need to organize a revolutionary movement, but one that will reject representative government per se, and seek to transform the entire social order, not just change the laws of the present one. Revolutionaries should probably just declare a moratorium on even discussing Democrats, Republicans, or Greens, beyond what is minimally necessary to know what is going on. We should instead concentrate on establishing real direct democracy in neighborhood, workplace, and household assemblies.

We must realize that *anarchy is the real nemesis to neoliberal capitalism*, both abroad (empire) and at home (fascism). Nothing short of this is a practical alternative. Nothing short of this can *win*. The era of representative government is over. Liberal democracies will never return. We will have fascism or anarchy. Those are our choices. This election proves that beyond any doubt. Bourgeois democracy cannot be fixed, nor is it worth fixing. But it requires a real leap to imagine a world without such structures of government. Nevertheless, it is a leap that we must make, now, with all the resources at our disposal. We are running out of time. But the historical opportunity is here. We must get this idea into the air. We must seize the time. The alternative is too awful to contemplate.

14

Capitalism and Transportation Infrastructure
(Random thoughts in assistance to a high school debater.)

May 2012

1 *First of all, in order to set the scene a bit*, it must be established that capitalism has been shaping our entire physical and social world for the past 500 years. Transportation is only one small part of it. By capitalism I mean a social order based on the profit-motive. The phrase "profit-motive" is just short-hand for "the accumulation of capital for the sake of accumulating capital" – which is a definition of capitalism. But it does this through maximizing profit, whether from production or financial speculation. Whenever the rate of profit falters in one arena (sector of the economy; geographical area), capital moves on. (More on this shortly.) Architecture and technology has been shaped by capitalist imperatives, as has land use, as are most of our institutions. Governments (the nation-state system) and capitalists are closely intertwined, embedded

Chapter 14

with each other. So our political institutions have been shaped by capitalists, to serve their own needs.

2. The expansion of capitalism has always been closely linked to the available means of transportation. In the first great expansion and founding of capitalism, from 1450 to 1650, the superiority of European sailing ships, combined with onboard ship cannons, enabled Europeans to conquer most of the coast lines of the world. Then the sailing ship was replaced by steam ships. Then came railroads, then autos and trucks, and finally airplanes. (A similar history could also be written about means of communication: from letters, to telegraph, to telephone, then radio and television, and now the internet.) The contemporary world could hardly exist as it is without the enormous supertankers, which enabled the transport of large quantities of oil cheaply. Such tankers are a relatively recent invention.

3. Another factor to consider is the source of energy. Although the earliest phases of industrialization were based on water power, this then shifted to coal and steam engines, which powered the great industrial revolutions of the 19th century. But for the past 150 years capitalist expansion has been based on oil, cheap oil. The entire vast capitalist world society we are living in at present would not be possible were it not for cheap oil. And cheap oil is coming to an end. God only knows what will happen when it does. This dependency is especially close as regards transportation: jet fuel (basically kerosene) for airplanes, diesel for trucks, buses, trains, and ships, and gasoline for cars. Oil is the most incredible energy source ever discovered, and it is running out. What has happened to us, is like what happens to any species when it suddenly finds itself with an inexhaustible supply of food and with no enemies – it expands exponentially. With us, the discovery of this energy source coincided with an existing social order which needed to grow incessantly or cease to exist, namely,

capitalism (accumulation of capital, maximization of profit). Eighty percent of the physical infrastructure in the United States (buildings, roads, everything material) has been built since the Second World War. This is true also for most of the world. But nothing can grow indefinitely. Cancer tries to do that but it eventually kills its host. Capitalism (a cancerous social order) is on the verge of killing the earth (its host). This is why it so urgent for us to stop it.

4. As for train transportation, Europe has a highly developed train system with many high-speed trains. The United States does not. Yet Europe is capitalist too. But Europe had very strong labor unions, and strong socialist and communist movements. These movements forced the governments there to set up the welfare state, wherein governments did a lot to improve the lives of ordinary people. Along with that came government investment in transportation. Japan has some high-speed trains too, and it is also capitalist. But there as well the tradition is for government to take a strong hand in the capitalist economy and its expansion. The United States never had such strong labor and socialist movements. It has been the most capitalist country in the world. Nevertheless, the interstate highway system was built by the government in the 1950s and 60s, mainly to facilitate capitalist expansion.

5. A peculiar thing happened in the United States, however, namely, the great streetcar conspiracy. Between the two world wars, the auto companies and the oil companies conspired to destroy the nation's urban streetcar system (see reference below). The highway construction industry also played a part in this. This paved the way for the transportation system to be based mostly on cars, buses, trucks, and planes – all of which use more oil and other materials than trains do. It also paved the way for the construction of suburbia, an automobile dependent residential development. It is practically impossible to live in suburbia without a car – no way to get to work, go buy groceries, visit

friends across town, or do anything or go anywhere without a car (since most cities have very inadequate bus systems).Autos and oil thus became key growth sectors (and a key source of profit) for the capitalist economy for a good many decades.

6. Suburbia was the ideal capitalist development. Each little family had their own house which had to be filled up with stuff – creating an incredible market for capitalist goods. Plus you had to have a car, or two or three cars. Plus it more or less destroyed community. And capitalists hate community. Suburbia created an atomized population. Isolated individuals are weaker than communities, and are less capable of resisting their exploitation.

7. I think it is highly unlikely that high speed trains will ever be built in the United States. They weren't built back when they should have been, during the heyday of US capitalism, during the boom years. So why would they be built now? What is happening now is that the transportation infrastructure is being allowed to decay. Hardly any money is going into its upkeep or improvement. Why? Because capitalism is abandoning the United States. The US is rapidly losing its hegemonic status in the world system. The center of capitalism is shifting to China, and elsewhere (e.g., Brazil, India), but mostly to China. This has happened five times in the past. Venice was a precursor hegemon. Then Genoa, Amsterdam, London, New York. These were the great centers (hegemons) of capitalist expansion. (For an account of this history, see the Giovanni Arrighi reference below). Even within a country you can have shifts in the center of production. Thus in the US we now have the "rustbelt" – Northeast and Midwest – formerly the center of industry, but now abandoned, left lying in ruins, as production shifted to the Southwest. This process of building up and then abandoning is entirely normal to capitalism. China, India, and Brazil are all engaged in

mammoth construction projects, just like the US did fifty years ago – highways, bridges, tunnels, dams, cities, railroads, and cars, cars, cars.

One trend might counter this somewhat and lead to the refurbishing of the rail system, namely, very expensive oil. If it gets prohibitively expensive to transport goods by truck, trains might make a comeback. But this will be freight trains, not passenger trains. High speed trains are for passengers, not freight.

― ― ―

Resources and References
Wikipedia, *Car Free Movement*
> http://en.wikipedia.org/wiki/Car-free_movement
> Many references to critiques of car culture, or google "carfree" for other references

The General Motors Streetcar Conspiracy
> http://en.wikipedia.org/wiki/General_Motors_streetcar_conspiracy or google "streetcar conspiracy" for other references.

Bikes Not Bombs
> http://bikesnotbombs.org/

Wikipedia, *History of Transport*
> http://bikesnotbombs.org/or google "history of transportation" for other references

End of Suburbia – 52 minute documentary on peak oil
> http://www.youtube.com/watch?v=Q3uvzcY2Xug

Wallerstein, Immanuel, *Historical Capitalism*.
> For a good, brief introduction to how capitalism works.

Arrighi, Giovanni, *The Long Twentieth Century*.
> Best general history of the 500-year-old social order known as capitalism (the book is mis-titled).

Herod, James, "Capitalists, Global Warming, and the
    Climate Justice Movement," on my website: <www.
    jamesherod.info> For a discussion of the prospects of
    stopping capitalists, who are on the verge of killing
    the earth.
Ward, Colin, *Freedom to Go: After the Motor Age.*
    London: Freedom Press, 1991, 112 pages.
    An anarchist considers transportation. Many
    references to trains, transportation, and the critique
    of the automobile.

— — —

Suggested propositions to debate:
** The Proift-Motive, as a way of organizing production,
    results in the greatest public good.
** Capitalists will save life on earth from being killed by
    global warming.
** Alternative sources of clean energy will allow us to
    replace fossil fuels and pretty much continue living as
    we now do in a highly industrialized and technological
    civilization.
** There Is No Alternative to Capitalism.

15

A Response to a Letter by Mr. Paul Weyrich

[A letter dated February 16, 1999, addressed to "Dear Friend," which was circulated on the web. My response, now edited for general circulation, was originally a reply to the friend who sent it to me. At the time, I had never heard of Paul Weyrich, which shows how little attention I had paid to this dimension of national life and politics, because I have since learned that he is a major figure on the Christian Right.]

February 1999

A friend emailed to me a letter by Mr. Paul Weyrich, thinking that I would find it interesting, because I had recommended abandoning ruling class institutions, in my book *Getting Free*, and Weyrich is seemingly saying something similar. Weyrich recommends withdrawing from mainstream culture, since he has become disillusioned with politics, because even though they (Christian conservatives) were successful, and got their people elected, and gained a lot of power in government, their social program remains unfulfilled.

There is a world of difference, however, between my proposal and his. I recommend pulling out of, abandoning, or gutting ruling class institutions as a way of overthrow-

Chapter 15

ing the ruling class, and establishing democratic communities which control their own destinies. This is a confrontational approach. Its aim is to destroy wage-slavery and hence the profit-motive and to restructure the entire world along different lines and according to different principles. I explicitly reject 'dropping out' (see Chapter 5, Strategies That Have Failed, page 34, in *Getting Free*).

Mr. Weyrich's proposal is instead an escapist approach. He wants to leave mainstream institutions in order to get away from them, to escape, so that he and others can live like they want to elsewhere. It is the standard Christian idea of being 'in the world but not of it,' and it is a strategy that has been followed again and again by utopian (religious and secular) communities throughout American and European history. It has never worked, because capitalism is a global structure, and has been from its beginnings in the long sixteenth century (1450-1650). Even isolated communities are still connected to this structure in important ways. You can see this still happening almost every day, as the few remaining isolated tribes in New Guinea, the Kalahari, or the Amazon are absorbed into the world market (in the best of cases; usually they are simply obliterated). But Mr. Weyrich is rather mild even in his escapist fantasies. He doesn't want anyone to go as far even as the Amish have in withdrawing from the surrounding society. He is simply seeking ways to protect himself and like-minded people from being "infected" by a decadent culture. He suggests home schooling, turning off the tv, boycotting Disney, avoiding videos and computer garbage, and so forth. Far from trying to overthrow an evil system, he is looking for "some sort of quarantine" from the "cultural rot."

He wants people to withdraw from the "culture." Will they also quit their jobs? He never once mentions the economy, or corporations, in this letter. He uses the word 'greed' only once, and in a very general way. He talks about a 'cultural war' having been fought and lost. He mentions the academic community, cultural institutions, the entertainment industry, but he is completely blind to the largest, wealthiest, most pervasive, most dominating institutions in American life, institutions all of us have contact with daily, almost hourly – corporations. (His opposition to Disney is because it is anti-religious and anti-Christian, and not because it is a corporation per se, let alone that it is monopolistic and imperialistic.) And this of course shows the weakness of the strategy. The idea that a community of people could live the way they want to without getting control of the land they live on and their workplaces (not to mention their schools, hospitals, banks, police, community governments) is ludicrous. Even in the nineteenth century, when such communities *could* control their land and most of their community institutions, they were still deeply embedded in the surrounding profit-oriented market, the surrounding national legal system (created by capitalists), the surrounding labor market, and so forth. These connections worked to severely restrict the autonomy of these communities.

What is most distressing, and incredible, to me is that Mr. Weyrich blames this "ever-widening sewer," this cultural disintegration and degradation, on the radicals of the sixties, on cultural Marxism, the Frankfurt school, on Herbert Marcuse, on "an alien ideology, an ideology bitterly hostile to Western culture." This claim is so preposterous it is hard to even know how to respond to it, but I'll try. (It is a claim, I might add, that has been financed by millions of dollars from America's corporate rich and propagated for the past thirty years in order to discredit and stigmatize the revolts of the sixties.)

To begin with, 'Political Correctness' was not invented by radicals, marxists, anarchists, or leftists. It is a phrase, or rather a whole political campaign, invented by conservatives, as a way of attacking the left. Insistence on political correctness is what leftists were accused of by conservatives. It was directed mainly against the few radicals who had managed to get hired by universities in the seventies,

Chapter 15

after the revolts of the sixties had opened up these institutions a little bit. Radicals in the universities never amounted to more than a few thousand professors out of nearly a million teachers nationwide. The right-wing attack on "political correctness" was a really vicious campaign, with an enormous outpouring of books and broadcasts, with the result that many left-leaning teachers lost their jobs. Mr. Weyrich complains that "you might even lose your job or be expelled from college" for saying the wrong thing. If you check the statistics, you will find that it was radicals, almost always, who were fired, not conservatives. By the late nineties, there are very few radicals left in the universities. Yet the ROTC is there big time, as are corporations, with the CIA recruiting on every campus. So Mr. Weyrich's claim that "It [political correctness] has taken over the academic community" is so far from the truth as to be laughable.

Eventually a few well written responses by radicals were published. One of the best is by Russell Jacoby, called, *Dogmatic Wisdom: How the Cultural Wars Divert Education and Distract America*. This book is worth examining if anyone wants to read the other side's (the left's) take on the issue. Actually, it is instructive to compare the deluge of conservative materials attacking the 'political correctness' of the left, with the paltry number of published responses the left has managed to get out. This shows the disproportionate level of power and wealth conservatives have in comparison to the left. The conservatives are financed by the Olin Foundation and a dozen other foundations. They have millions. They are bankrolled by some of the wealthiest families and corporations in America. They fund conservative newspapers on the campuses. They set up think tanks. Whereas radicals are invariably broke, and few in number. It is preposterous to think that radicals are taking over the country, the government, the media, the universities, or anything else.

Universities have always been rather tightly controlled

A Response to a Letter by Mr. Paul Weyrich

by the ruling class. After World War II the GI Bill enabled millions of ordinary Americans to go to college for the first time (and also there was a great expansion of higher education in state universities). But prior to this higher education was mostly for the sons and daughters of the rich. And now it is becoming that way again, and increasingly so, with the dramatic rise in the costs of tuition. In American history, there is just this one small window to higher education, for children of the poor, during the boom years after World War Two, when a substantial number of working class kids made it to college. I was fortunate to have lived when that small window was open for a brief period.

The really huge change in higher education during the past decades has been its takeover by large corporations. They have founded whole departments, financed departmental chairs, built institutes, bought research, and so forth. Many professors move back and forth between the corporate world and the university world. Whereas before, universities were *relatively* autonomous (from corporations as such, but never from the ruling class in general), now they are intimately linked with the corporate world. How anyone could believe that the academic world is controlled by 'cultural Marxists' is beyond me. Such a belief simply shows the ignorance, bias, and blindness with which the Christian right views the world.

Mr. Weyrich presumes that Marxism is alien and hostile to "Western culture," whereas in fact marxism, socialism, communism, and anarchism are part and parcel of Western culture (and to my mind, the highest expression of that culture). They are creations of western culture, and are as much a part of it as are the profit-motive, Mozart, science, the Catholic Church, or atheism. Socialism was a movement created by working people in Europe after having been driven off their peasant freeholds and turned into factory workers, a process they resisted fiercely.

And besides, the real attack on Christianity came not from Marxism, a nineteenth century movement, but much

Chapter 15

earlier, from the Enlightenment philosophers of the 17th and 18th centuries in Europe. Weyrich reveals his ignorance once again, and also his alignment with the corporate rich. Ever since the Bolshevik Revolution in Russia our capitalist rulers have been trying to blame all the evils of the world on communists rather than have their own sordid and greedy practices exposed as the culprit.

Mr. Weyrich complains that "for the first time in their lives, people have to be afraid of what they say." "Certain topics are forbidden." Once again his narrow-mindedness and shortsightedness shines through, because there have long been persons who had to be afraid of what they said. The main topic forbidden in the nation's schools and universities, not to mention cinema, tv, and radio, is any criticism of capitalism. Those persons who have rejected a social order whose fundamental law is the accumulation of capital, through profit, to the neglect of all other values, have always had to be afraid of what they said. They have been afraid because the dangers have been very real. They have been shot, hanged, beaten, fired, exiled, gassed, sued, and imprisoned, not to mention slandered and defamed. Weyrich complains that he doesn't want to be labeled a racist, sexist, or homophobic, just because he says something that is not considered 'politically correct.' Yet he has no problem labeling someone as an alien, or a degenerate. And of course conservatives in general are quick with judgmental, derogatory labels, the most popular being "terrorist," with "anarchist" rapidly coming back in as a favorite, now that "communist" is no longer historically viable as a smear. Even the term 'liberal' has been turned into a smear, so that people now refer to the "L-word."

If Weyrich knew a little more history, he would be thanking anarchists and communists for having fought for so many decades, from the Civil War to World War Two, to get in reality the First Amendment rights that were guaranteed to them by the Constitution. It was Emma Goldman, among others, who really won "freedom of speech" for all

A Response to a Letter by Mr. Paul Weyrich

Americans, not the founding fathers. Until this struggle for free speech, waged at great cost by radicals, the First Amendment was a dead letter. Now of course, those First amendment Rights are rapidly being stripped away once again by corporate America.

One of the most amazing things about this letter is that Weyrich, after admitting openly to having waged a thirty-year-long political campaign to take over the government, *and having succeeded*, in order to "implement our agenda," can then complain that the country is becoming an "ideological state" (referring to 'political correctness'). Fundamentalist Christianity, this "agenda" he was trying to "implement" (i.e., impose on the entire nation) is not thought of as an ideology I guess. His own beliefs are simply the truth, or "our traditional culture," whereas the beliefs of his opponents are an "ideology." So much for 'fairness in media' so avidly sought by the Christian right.

Mr. Weyrich speaks throughout this short letter about "our culture" or "our traditional culture." The arrogance of people like this always amazes me. How can they can presume to own the culture, or assume that their beliefs are the "culture" whereas everyone else's are "alien"? We sixties radicals encountered this attitude thirty years ago, repeatedly, when we started raising a few questions about what was happening in America. Conservatives said to us: "If you don't like this country, leave." They presumed to own the country, presumed that it was theirs, but not ours. It was their culture, but not ours. I was always especially infuriated by this attitude.

In this country, from the very beginning, there were slaves, eventually millions of them, who were not part of a "Judeo-Christian civilization;" so Weyrich implicitly excludes them from "our culture." Similarly, even after having suffered a war of extermination, there were still hundreds of thousands of Indians, eventually a million or more, living here. So he implicitly excludes all these people from "our traditional culture." And the truth is, for born-

Chapter 15

again Christians and the religious right, Jews are also excluded from "our culture." In spite of their use of the phrase "Judeo-Christian," anti-semitism is deeply embedded in fundamentalist Christianity, because the Jews rejected and killed Christ. Tens of millions of secular persons, who are not religious at all, are also excluded, in Mr. Weyrich's definition, from "our culture." Since the middle of the nineteenth century there have been millions of Chinese living here, who are mostly Buddhists, and now there are millions of Arabs, Turks, and Persians, who are mostly Muslims. None of these people are included in "our traditional culture." In short, his is an unbelievably arrogant and bigoted attitude.

Perhaps most insulting to me though was Mr. Weyrich's sentence: "The radicals of the 1960s had three slogans: turn on, tune in, and drop out." What a truly ignorant, weird, unbelievable distortion of one of the great revolts of the twentieth century. It was one of only two system-wide revolutions ever against capitalism, the other being in 1848. It was global in scope. It was primarily a rejection, by young people, of the prevailing 'affluent' or 'commodity' culture, that is, the materialism of a mature capitalism, and indeed, of its decadence. It was also overwhelmingly a revolt against authority, in favor of democracy. It was a blow for freedom, almost across the board, including (but not limited to, even though these later became the most famous) sexual, gender, and racial freedom. It was a revolt against fatuity and complacency. It was waged everywhere by the best and brightest, and the most moral, I might add. It was also an anti-war movement, that is, a strike for peace. It was a protest against the defilement of the environment. It was a strike against the stifling rigidities, hierarchies, and elite control of universities everywhere, and against the mendacity of those in authority, and against their complicity in crimes against humanity.

But already by the early seventies the counter-revolution had set in. The revolts were thoroughly crushed. And

A Response to a Letter by Mr. Paul Weyrich

then, for the next thirty years, we were vilified in every conceivable way by corporate media. Next to unions and the labor movement in general hardly any group in America is hated more by the ruling class than sixties radicals. They have spent many millions of dollars discrediting us. And of course their spin has been accepted by millions of people, including Mr. Weyrich.

What Mr. Weyrich, and the Christian right in general, think of as the 'left' is not the left at all, but only two or three elements of it which corporate America found palatable and therefore incorporated into the mainstream. Originally, the women, gay, and black movements were radical, in that they sought fundamental changes in the structure of American institutions. They were trying to overthrow the system, not just get into it, or at least a very significant segment of those movements were radical. But very rapidly, already by the McGovern campaign of 1972, each of these movements became overwhelmingly mainstream. They now sought only to get into the system, and reform it from within, rather than overthrow it. Do you think that feminists, gays, and blacks would have been allowed onto national television, which is completely owned and controlled by ruling corporations, if they had been a real threat to the establishment? Would Departments of Women's and African American studies have been set up in universities, which are completely controlled by the ruling class, if the establishment had seen these departments as threats? Do you ever see any pro-labor people on television, or any anti-capitalists? Do you ever hear anyone mention class, let alone the working class, on national television? A key feature of the new departments of women's and black studies is that class has been eliminated from their intellectual frameworks. They are strictly 'identity politics' people, not people involved in class struggle. These departments are there even so as mere appendages to the curriculum, are barely tolerated, and are very far from controlling the

Chapter 15

entire university as Weyrich claims.

Here were three movements, in their de-radicalized versions, which were entirely palatable to the ruling class. So they co-opted them. Or more accurately, they simply didn't resist them, since these reformists were there pounding on the doors of the establishment demanding to be let in. When corporate America really doesn't want to let people in you see a different response entirely: it ignores them, slanders them, impoverishes them, disempowers them, or simply kills them. So if Mr. Weyrich and the Christian right in general hate feminists, gays, and blacks so much, they must thank the ruling class itself for their presence in mainstream culture, not radicals from the sixties or cultural Marxism. As far as radicals are concerned, these movements long ago lost whatever revolutionary content they once had. In their mainstream versions, they have done very little to establish greater equality in American life. They have served mainly to legitimate the ruling class, to take the heat off it, and to give it a breather. The President can now say, "Look, I have a rainbow cabinet." Of course its members are all as rich as Croesus. (Even so, the ruling class is incredibly afraid of these movements in their radical versions.)

Weyrich complains that "it [political correctness] threatens to control literally every aspect of our lives." Talk about not living in the real world! At a time when billions of dollars have been spent to beef up police departments in every little town in America, when new linkages are being made every day, with computers, between these police departments and vehicle licensing bureaus, tax collectors, insurance agencies, and what have you (alimony enforcers), when the ruling class, through its corporations and governments, is tightening its controls and constraints on us unruly subjects on an almost daily basis, so that we can hardly move without it being recorded somewhere, on some list or in some bank or on some camera, Weyrich thinks that his life is being controlled by "political correctness." (Are the surveillance cameras in banks, on street corners, in libraries, and in department stores because of 'political correctness'?)

I guess it is the presence of feminists, blacks, and gays on national television and in movies, plus a few other hotly debated items, like abortion or school prayer, that leads Christian conservatives to believe that the country has been taken over by "aliens" and that they have lost the "cultural war." But how can they be blind to the overwhelmingly conservative character of the past quarter century – one of the most reactionary periods in American history? Beginning in the early 1970s the rich launched a very aggressive attack on the remnants of the New Left, on the paltry legislation the New Left had managed to get through Congress, on New Deal legislation itself, on labor unions, on welfare, on unemployment insurance, and now even on social security. The rich drastically reduced their own tax burden, won spectacular bailouts from the government which must be paid for by average people, siphoned off billions in subsidies for their corporations from the public treasury, bought public lands and public research for a song, wiped safety regulations practically off the books, gutted civil liberties with draconian anti-crime and anti-terrorist bills, gave pharmaceuticals a free hand, destroyed or co-opted the environmental movement, built hundreds of new prisons, turned the CIA loose on America (thinking I guess that the police and FBI needed help), gave the Pentagon a blank check, eliminated independent newspapers and publishing houses, cleared the way for irradiated meat and genetically modified food, and even pushed through treaties which nullify the sovereignty of the government itself vis-a-vis global corporations. And Christian conservatives believe that this has been a period of history controlled by cultural Marxists? Unbelievable!

How can anyone not see that the cultural disintegration or collapse about which he complains so bitterly is the result of the normal functioning of a profit-oriented society, of its unrelenting attack on communities everywhere, on all things not yet commodified, on all values and relationships not yet fractured through the lens of 'profit for profit's sake,' on all persons and peoples who resist the logic of the market? Just look at any town, at the 'mall'-ification of America, at the emptying of the countryside, at the abandonment of schools, parks, and public libraries. What kind of evidence does it take to indict a system, I'd like to know?

Weyrich had wanted to "re-take the cultural institutions" (notice he never mentions economic institutions) that are now "controlled by the enemy." (Now I guess he only wants to escape from them.) The problem is that he has mis-identified the enemy. He has zero comprehension of the structure of power in the country. And thus he plays into the hands of our corporate rulers (if he is not deliberately and consciously in bed with them). He attacks all the wrong people. Or, from a ruling class point of view, he attacks exactly the right people.

So much for Mr. Weyrich's take on the problems that plague us. At least he admits that the majority of people in America do not share his beliefs. Radicals had a bumper sticker for a while that said "The Moral Majority Is Neither." It was always clear to everyone but the Christian right itself that the extremely puritanical social mores and agenda which it sought to implement was a minority program.

I believe that Christian conservatives, most of whom are average persons, everyday Americans, have merely been used by the right wing of the ruling class as a smoke screen behind which to push its pro-rich, neo-liberal, corporate agenda. Here was a ready-made movement involving millions of Americans, and very frustrated and angry Americans at that. So our rich rulers poured millions of dollars into this movement, and then under the guise of fighting for good clean Christian values they pushed through some of the most oppressive and regressive legislation in American history. Try to remember that **Money** is the one true religion of the rich and powerful.

Can any common ground be found between Christian conservatives and radicals like myself? Quite frankly, it's hard to imagine finding any common grounds with the likes of Jesse Helms, Pat Robertson, or Jerry Falwell, who are really vicious and bigoted persons. But what about ordinary persons? We do disapprove of many of the same things, and there are a few common elements in our pictures of how we would like to live. But our analyses of the causes of our problems, our conceptions of who the enemy is, and our ideas of what to do about all this, are worlds apart. It might be easier for persons like myself to find common grounds with more secular, so-called 'populist' types, that is, with right-wing libertarians, than with conservative Christians. Right-wing libertarianism is after all a predominant belief system in America. I will continue to ponder this question of trying to find some grounds for a dialogue with all these millions.

So there you have it, two irreconcilable agendas. Mr. Weyrich seeks to implement his, I seek to implement mine. Of the two though, mine is the more tolerant, humane, and civilized. There is after all room in my society for people like him (up to a point), whereas there is none in his for people like me (at any point). Except for a few fragile revolutionary religious flowers which have bloomed here and there, the religious throughout history have sided overwhelmingly with the ruling classes of the world, and thus have contributed mightily for millennia to the oppression of humanity.

16
Indigenism: A Critique

August, 2001

*T**his is actually the same issue* as the nationalities question and the identity question, but it might be worthwhile to treat it separately because there is an outstanding Native-American writer, Ward Churchill, who develops and advocates this theory. It is a theory, of native or indigenous peoples, which tends to replace class analysis, and generates a view of the history of the last five hundred years of world history which is quite at odds with an understanding of capitalism. I have never seen a critique of the idea (although surely some marxist journal has published one).

It is quite erroneous to identify the enemy as Western Civilization, Europeans, or White People and to attribute the world's problems to these false abstractions. The rise and spread of capitalism was not only massively resisted by peoples all over the world, generating brilliant articulations of this resistance by writers and leaders like Fanon, James, Cabral, Nkrumah, Gandhi, Magon, Mandela, and Cesaire. It was also resisted by Europeans themselves. The European peasants were among the first so-called indigenous or native peoples to be dispossessed and colonized by the emerging capitalist ruling class. They were driven off their lands and forced into wage-slavery. Their villages were destroyed, and their local cultures, as were their

Chapter 16

unique languages.

European resistance to capitalism was vigorous and long lasting. It gave rise to massive movements: the labor movement, the cooperative movement, communism, socialism, anarchism, syndicalism. It resulted in revolutions: the revolutions of 1848, the Paris Commune, the failed revolutions in Central Europe in 1919, the Spanish Civil War, the Hungarian Revolution of 1956, Polish Solidarity, and so forth. There was a worldwide upsurge of anti-capitalist resistance in 1968, and this took place also throughout Europe and the West. Recently there has been another such wave of global opposition to capitalism, but which has appeared also in Seattle, Quebec City, and Genoa. Thus I believe that Indigenism mis-identifies the enemy, and is therefore incompatible with an Association of Free Peoples (anarchism, communism).

Actually, we are just now witnessing a still basically peasant population in Europe, in the Balkans, being hit with an improved, strengthened, new, enclosures movement. Are the peasants in twenty-first century Eastern Europe indigenous peoples who are being attacked by Western Civilization or are they being dispossessed by the neoliberal offensive of late capitalism? Indigenists I think will have to be double-jointed to apply their theory to recent events in Eastern Europe, because peasants there are White, European, a part of Western Civilization, and are Indigenous, if by that term we mean that they have lived there for eons (although most of them moved there from elsewhere in some distant past, as have all so-called Indigenous peoples on earth). So I guess they are attacking themselves, if we follow Indigenism.

Thus, rejection of and resistance to capitalism, imperialism, and colonialism has been going on in Europe too, not just in the world outside Europe. It distorts the picture to deny this. Marx himself wrote some of the earliest analyses of colonialism in his essays on India and Ireland. Western Civilization thus includes not only capitalism, but also the critique of capitalism. If we use the term at all it should include both these movements, the evil of capitalism and the good of anti-capitalism. It includes not only White Europeans who fought to impose capitalism on the world, but White Europeans who fought to stop this and to get free from capitalism completely. The terms European and White are false abstractions, in that it is only some Europeans and only some Whites that have colonized the world. Just as it was wrong for some radical feminists to see all men as the enemy, or for some black nationalists to see all whites as the enemy, so also it is wrong for Native Americans to see all non-indigenous people as the enemy, and for Indigenists to blame all Europeans and all Whites for imperialism.

Thus I can no longer accept the notion of indigenous versus nonindigenous people. I much prefer to think in terms of oppressors and the oppressed, exploiters and the exploited, criminals and victims, rulers and the ruled, rather than in terms of western civilization versus the rest of the world, and certainly rather than Whites versus People of Color. Ireland, one of the first countries to be colonized, was a nation of white people.

In Africa, the ruling classes are Africans, in the Middle East they are Arabs, Turks, Persians, or Jews, in Asia they are Asians. Local ruling classes, generally speaking, are of the race and ethnicity of their nations, and yet are intimately tied into the world capitalist system, vigorously defend it, and use it to exploit their peoples, for their own enrichment. Japanese exploit Japanese in Japan, Chinese exploit Chinese in China, Indians exploit Indians in India, Haitians exploit Haitians in Haiti. So how can it be claimed that oppressors are all European and White?

It has even become fashionable now to criticize anyone who talks of Capitalism as having originated in Europe and spread from there throughout the world as Eurocentric. Why anyone would want to take credit for an evil social order like capitalism is a mystery to me. But as has been

Chapter 16

recently argued brilliantly by Ellen Meiksins Wood, their anti-Eurocentrism is itself Eurocentric, in that it embraces a liberal European theory about the origins of capitalism, as having evolved naturally from trade and commerce (basically, the Pirenne thesis), which evolution would have happened elsewhere had it not been blocked by Europeans, rather than adopt the radical analysis which claims that capitalism originated in an unusual set of historical circumstances and is not a natural development at all, but an aberration. This widespread anti-Eurocentrism is on a par with the growing influence of Indigenism, and is just as misguided.

I argue, however, that in point of fact, seen historically, there is no such thing as an indigenous people. Every people on earth originally came from somewhere else. Even Africans who are now living in the very same area where our species first appeared came from somewhere else, because those original homo sapiens are long gone, having migrated to the far corners of the earth. Those living there now moved in from elsewhere. Reports are, that of the Indians now living in Chiapas, Mexico, a lot of them moved there recently from Guatemala. All the so-called native peoples of the Americas of course originally came from somewhere else, either from Siberia (the traditional theory) or from across the seas (Cyrus Gordon). I've never heard anyone claim that homo sapiens evolved independently in the Americas.

There have been mass migrations throughout human history – Huns moving into eastern Europe, Turks from Central Asia moving into the fertile crescent and Asia Minor, Aztecs conquering the Mayans, Vikings settling in Ireland, Normans invading England, Russians migrating into Siberia, Greeks into Asia Minor, Franks and Celts filtering south into the Roman Empire, Arabs into Spain, Chinese into Indonesia, Jews into Palestine, Africans into the Americas, Indians into South Africa, and on and on.

Indigenism: A Critique

The human race is one incredibly jumbled up affair.

A people has always called itself something, always has had a name for itself, which is one thing we mean by ethnicity. But the more general concept of indigenous people is of more recent origin. In fact I believe it is of very recent origin, dating from the sixties. I think it is part of the Identity Politics that emerged out of the New Left in the United States. The New Left, in its determined blindness to the working class, invented a whole set of new categories, and built movements on them – women, gays and lesbians, blacks, old people, welfare mothers, youth, Latinos – and, of course, Native Americans. There was a movement here, AIM, the American Indian Movement, of which Leonard Peltier was a member. Native Americans became one of the many categories (replacing that of class) that made up Identity Politics. Fortunately, we are currently witnessing, after nearly thirty dreary years, the demise of this orientation. Not to say that there weren't positive things accomplished by this focus, but it couldn't, and didn't, overthrow capitalism.

Obviously, the idea of an indigenous people sets up a contrast with non-indigenous peoples. And in our present historical situation we all know who that refers to – Europeans. We certainly never see it used with regard to the Japanese colonizing Southeast Asia, or the Chinese colonizing Tibet. No, it is a current, but badly misguided, attempt to conceptualize the expansion of capitalism to all corners of the earth. This is actually a mis-conceptualization, because it blames all Europeans for something that only a few of them have done. It sets up a conflict between Europeans and the rest of humanity, ignoring the fact that European peasants were among the first to be colonized, dispossessed, uprooted, and sent packing, as well as ignoring the fact that local ruling classes have helped affix the ball and chain of capitalism to every nook and cranny of the earth.

We must remember that the great migrations of peo-

Chapter 16

ple out of Europe that have taken place under capitalism were not all composed of imperialists and colonizers. Many of those leaving were such, of course, but they were very far from being in the majority. Australia was founded as a prison colony. The ruling class of England expelled its criminals and undesirables from England and deposited them in Australia. Millions came to the United States as indentured servants. Tens of millions more came as the result of the enclosures movement in Europe. They had been forced off their lands and had to go elsewhere to live. Blacks of course were brought here as slaves (and it's interesting that Blacks are never considered, by Indigenists, as non-indigenous people, no matter where they live; this is a slur that is reserved for European whites). The great wave of Irish immigration to this country was caused by the colonization of Ireland by the English, who seized the farms there and used them for export crops, thus starving millions of Irish peasants, who had to leave – a process that is going on now again all over the world on a vast scale. Millions of eastern European Jews came to this country to escape the pogroms, in 1905 especially, but also at other times. The vast migrations to Brazil, Argentina, Uruguay, and Paraguay were for similar reasons.

When we start thinking in terms of indigenous versus non-indigenous, native versus European, people of color versus whites, we get into such a briar patch of contradictions it becomes simply laughable. Are the whites in South Africa, who have been there for four hundred years, to pack up and go back to Europe, because they are not indigenous? (Same with Algeria, Canada, Australia, New Zealand, the United States.) Are the nations of Argentina, Uruguay, and Paraguay, which are predominantly of European extract and white, to be defined as People of Color and Third World? Are the Irish, one of the first people colonized, included in the oppressed indigenous peoples, or are they white Europeans and part of the oppressors? Are the Turks, many of whom look just like Europeans, with red hair and all, being of Indo-European stock mixed up with Mongolian stock, people of color or white? Are they part of Asia or Europe? Are they third world or first world? They nearly conquered Vienna once, after all, and have lived in the Balkans for half a millennium. Should the Puerto Ricans in New York, Turks in Berlin, Algerians in Paris, Chinese in San Francisco, or West Indians in London all go back where they came from? Are the Chinese communities in Indonesia indigenous or not? Are the Indian communities in South Africa indigenous or not? Are the Arabs in the southern Sahara to go back to Arabia where they came from? How long does a people have to live in an area before it becomes indigenous? Do the Jews (the Zionists among them), who want to go 'home' to Palestine, have a real claim to that territory even though they have been gone for 2000 years and Arabs have been living there all that time? Can they now go back and drive the Arabs out, claiming that Palestine is theirs? How anyone can think that this quagmire is superior to class analysis is beyond me.

A critic of my take on indigenism said that I had missed the point. Indigenous is just a name for the people who were in a place before the Europeans arrived, he claimed. Perhaps the concept has a certain plausibility when applied to the United States and Canada, and one or two other places, but it rapidly breaks down if applied worldwide (and it is even false, as explained above, when used for the US and Canada). Yet Indigenism is being applied worldwide, and has practically become a movement, and is spreading, as an analysis, and becoming a widely accepted approach to the strategy and philosophy of revolution.

Naturally, if there are important grass roots movements of people who call themselves indigenous you might argue that it makes sense to call them what they themselves call themselves, and for the most part I would agree. Of course, a movement, group, or people can call themselves anything they want to. It is their right to do so. And out of respect for them, there is generally no reason

Chapter 16

why others shouldn't accept the name. That doesn't mean we have to suspend critical judgement though, especially if a name has theoretical significance. I had no problem, for example, switching from Negro to African-American, because in that case, it was pretty much immaterial to me what name was preferred. (I refuse to use the term People of Color however, which I regard as pompous, euphemistic, and pretentious, seeing no difference between it and Colored People, which is taboo; the condoned phrase is actually closely linked with Indigenism).

The term indigenous however is in a rather different category. It has become a name for a whole analysis, an analysis which is unaware of or denies that we live in a capitalist social order. So I'm wary of it, and ultimately opposed to it. None of this means however that I don't support the revolts of people who call themselves indigenous, like the Zapatista revolt in Chiapas, which is obviously a very significant struggle. All kinds of struggles are undertaken by people who don't have the analysis that I wish they had – strikes, boycotts, urban insurrections, demonstrations – all done by people who don't have a thought of overthrowing capitalism – but I'm happy to see those revolts. It will all add up in the end, or at least I hope so. The Zapatistas have been especially creative in breaking down all sorts of barriers, mind sets, categories, and boundaries. Who knows where it will all end? It's hard to imagine that it won't end in something good. But I still take a critical attitude toward their conceptual framework and self-identity.

I recently asked a friend who is living in Mexico about the racial breakdown in Mexico, and whether or not there was a name for a pure blooded Spaniard, and how conscious people were of racial distinctions there. He sent me back some passages from a book by James Cockcroft, Mexico's Hope, which described the following distinctions (this was from considerably earlier in Mexican history): "Spaniards were at the top of the social pyramid, followed by successful criollos (whites born in Mexico), mestizos (of mixed Span-

Indigenism: A Critique

ish/Indian descent), mulattos (of mixed black and white descent), negros (Africans), and, at the bottom, Indians." (There are obviously a couple of likely categories missing: persons of mixed black and indian descent, and persons of mixed white, black, and indian decent.) So the question is: how can a mix like this ever be divided into indigenous and non-indigenous, and even if it could be, how could a just social policy ever be based on such a distinction?

In Cuba, the people who lived on the island before Columbus have long since been exterminated. None of the people there now are indigenous (in the sense of being there before Columbus). The population of Cuba now is composed of ex-slaves (blacks, negroes), ex-slave owners and other Spaniards (whites, criollos), and mulattos. Indigenists though do not consider the population of Cuba to be non-indigenous (a bad term), but third world and people of color (good terms). So their application of the concept is rather contradictory and hypocritical.

The Turks started migrating into Asia Minor around the eleventh century. They captured Constantinople in 1453. So I guess you couldn't consider them indigenous to Anatolia, having come originally from Central Asia, although by now they have been living there for nine hundred years.

North Africa, originally a land of the Berbers, was overrun first by Arabs, and then by Ottoman Turks, and finally by the French, as empires waxed and waned. The Berbers, Arabs, Turks, and French are all still there.

In Lebanon, the population is divided religiously into Marionite Christians, Druses, and Muslims, all ethnic Arabs, plus hundreds of thousands of Palestinian refugees, from just across the border. Are the Palestinian refugees non-indigenous? They are Arabs, but not Lebanese. Each of the main religious groups considers the others as somewhat illegitimate, although not exactly alien or foreign I guess. At one time or another, since ancient times, just about every ethnic group in the Middle East, and there are many, has passed through Lebanon, with some of them

Chapter 16

staying behind to settle. It would be next to impossible to say who is indigenous to that region. In Egypt, in the Nile delta, peasants have been there for eons. I guess you could call them indigenous.

Of course, European Spaniards are themselves mestizos in a sense, being a mixture of Arab and European genes (and Arabs are a mixture of Indo-European, Mongolian, and African genes). In this case, since the Arabs were the invading group, representing a so-called higher civilization, and were imposing their culture on so-called native, indigenous Europeans, the Spaniards were the colonized, while the Arabs were the colonizers. So many contemporary Spaniards are mestizos, the descendants of a colonized people, who intermarried with their colonizers.

The same might be said of the Turkish invasion of Eastern Europe and the Balkans. The Turks were the invaders. So the Europeans, according to indigenous theory, would have to be considered the native, indigenous, colonized element. There was also an earlier invasion of Eastern Europe by the Huns from Central Asia (c.379), and a later invasion by Mongolians (c.1279).

Also, many southern Europeans have some African genes, from way back, and are therefore mulattos. Dark complexioned persons are born throughout Europe in fact, except in the far north. Marx was called The Moor because of his dark complexion. So, many eastern and southern Europeans have long been either mestizos or mulattos. All of which shows why I believe it is rather absurd to try to comprehend history in terms of blood lines.

Many radical Latinos who are part European genetically, nevertheless adopt the identity of an indigenous person. How is it that they identify only with their Indian genes, but not with their European genes? Isn't it somewhat dishonest not to acknowledge one's actual genetic heritage, but instead only recognize those genes that are ideologically fashionable?

I got into a dispute once with a man who walked into

the Lucy Parsons Center, a radical bookstore in Boston, and started trashing a young woman who was staffing the store, because she was white, and therefore imperialist, and "part of the problem". This man himself was white. He looked European to me. I could see no visible evidence of black or indian genes. It turned out though that he was Puerto Rican, and considered himself to be a Person of Color. It's possible of course that he was Mestizo or Mulatto, and might have fathered black or brown children. But it's also possible that he was a pure-blooded descendant of Spaniards, and of pure European ancestry, genetically speaking. Yet he denied the European part of his genetic heritage.

There was another similar incident at the store one day. A young woman came in who claimed that she was an Indian. She was tall and slender, had blue eyes, blond hair, and ivory white skin. I looked at her in astonishment. "How do you figure that?" I asked her. She claimed that her great-great grandmother was an Indian. So we see how far at least one sensitive young person would go to avoid the stigma of being White and European, a stigma that has been aided and abetted by Indigenism.

A big part of the problem with the concept of indigenous people is that it is linked to territory in a very bad way. Can the remaining American Indians in the United States ever really be free by trying to reclaim the land they once lived on? Can they link their destiny to the reservations they still own (by treaty with the government in Washington, DC)? Or is another approach called for, in which all peoples can be free, regardless of their ethnicity or where they live, and where nothing, including land, is commodified and bought and sold?

Edward Said published an insightful piece recently in the *Progressive* (December 1999), about territory, although I don't think he got it quite right. He had returned to a village in Palestine, where a horrible massacre of Palestinians had taken place in 1948, and was struck by the irreconcil-

Chapter 16

able interpretations of the place offered by himself and his Israeli guide. He writes:

"This incident raises a profound existential dilemma, and not just for Palestinians: how to deal with issues of contested territory and competing claims of ethno-national identity?

"It seems clear to me that schemes of separation and partition and wishful ideas of creating ethnic or religious homogeneity have failed miserably and, in fact, have reproduced and intensified the problems they were designed to remedy. The idea was to divide Ireland between Protestants and Catholics. It hasn't worked. The idea to divide Cyprus between Turks and Greeks hasn't worked, either. The partition of Palestine between Jews and Arabs hasn't worked. Israel is not a homogeneous Jewish state. Twenty percent of the population are non-Jews. What do you do about them? The whole idea of partitioning and trying to separate ethnic groups who have lived together in one way or another, in contest or not, into pure states is a mistake. Look at India, which is largely a Hindu state but has a Muslim population of 120 to 150 million people. What do you do about them?"

Later on, he describes, rightly, the destruction that Identity Politics has caused in the Middle East over most of the decades of his life. And then he comments: "Identity, I think, is more of a burden and an inhibitor of thought – especially identity as ethnic, religious, or even national particularity. This identity strikes me as something to be gotten over." Unfortunately, though, in seeking a solution to "the ravages of the politics of identity", he moves in the direction of a universal, secular humanism, rather than toward a decentered, diverse, anarchistic world. If he had given more consideration to the two-hundred-year-old communist and anarchist attack on states as such, he might have seen another solution.

17
Defeating Capitalists Quickly to Save the Earth

December 2016

How we can defeat capitalists quickly? Why quickly? Because we have run out of time. Capitalists are on the verge of killing most life on earth, including humans, with global warming. This essay will present some exploratory thoughts on this dire situation we find ourselves in, especially with regard to our anti-capitalist struggles, our hopes for anarchy, and our prospects for cooling the earth. This is only a sketch; it will take a lot of work to flesh it out, probably more than I will be able to do.

We are way past the time when getting off fossil fuels could have alleviated global warming. If a determined, concerted effort had been made forty years ago by the governments of the world when James Hansen first alerted the president and Congress of the United States of the dangers of the excessive buildup of carbon dioxide in the atmosphere, getting off fossil fuels would probably have averted the severe crisis we now face.[1] But now? Our only option

---

[1] James Hansen recounts his efforts to alert the government in Chapters 1-3 in his book, *Storms of My Grandchildren: The Truth about the Coming Climate Catastrophe and Our Last Chance to Save Humanity*. New York: Bloomsbury, 2009, 304 pages.

Chapter 17

now is to find ways to remove carbon dioxide and other green house gases from the atmosphere. This has to be done now, immediately, and fast, because there is already enough CO2 in the atmosphere to melt the frozen Arctic.

It is estimated that there are 1700 gigatons (a gigaton is a billion tons) of methane stored in the shallow Arctic continental shelf, and another 1750 gigatons trapped in the frozen tundra all across Siberia and northern Canada.[2] There are at present only 5 gigatons of methane in the atmosphere. The unfrozen methane is already being released. A few years ago Scandinavian and Russian teams studying this found several plumes a few hundred feet wide bubbling up along the Siberian Arctic coast. Now the plumes are one kilometer wide, and there are hundreds of them. Some scientists are fearful that 50 gigatons could be released rather quickly in the near future, much of it perhaps even in a great burp, which would warm the earth further, causing the release of even more methane, in a self-reinforcing feedback loop. The earth could become very hot within just two or three decades. Eventually, the atmosphere could even become poisonous to life, like the atmosphere of Venus, although that is probably down the road a bit.[3]

The methane threat is the most serious of the imminent threats to life from global warming. Another very serious one is the acidification and warming of the oceans, which is killing marine life. Forty percent of the plankton is already gone. The ocean is losing its oxygen. A dead ocean is probably incompatible with the continuation of life on earth. Many climate scientists do not see our situation

---

[2] These figures are taken from Paul Beckwith's YouTube videos on global warming in the fall of 2016, the recent six-part summary of the scientific evidence, "Rapid Climate Change & Impacts for Environmental Assessment." Part 1 begins at:
<https://www.youtube.com/watch?v=C1Pr_tAKs6E>.
Beckwith is an expert Canadian climate scientist. He has many YouTube videos on the climate crisis.

[3] See Chapter 10, "The Venus Syndrome," in James Hansen, *Storms of My Grandchildren*.

as being quite as dire as I'm saying it is, but they may be underestimating the methane threat. I have been following the reports of the scientists studying the Arctic methane. They are all quite alarmed.

So here is the absolutely terrible bind we are in. Almost every proposal for cooling the earth would require massive, coordinated, global efforts by most governments of the world. Yet these governments are mostly controlled by capitalists. Capitalists are causing global warming. They put profit ahead of life. As a result, governments have failed for forty years to take any effective action to halt or reduce global warming.

For example, one proposal for removing CO_2 from the atmosphere, suggested years ago, is reforestation. For this to be effective, it would have to be a massive, planet-spanning, international campaign. Instead, the remaining forests are being cut down at a rapid clip. Or again, it might be possible to build a factory that could remove CO_2 from the air (much more than is used to build and run the factory). These factories could then be mass produced and installed all over the planet. This would take enormous resources. Under present arrangements, only governments could undertake such a campaign. Similarly with a proposal advanced more recently, that a shift to organic, small-scale, sustainable agriculture would remove CO_2 from the atmosphere. This would require the defeat of global agribusiness and industrial agriculture. Paul Beckwith, the eminent Canadian climate scientist, has proposed setting off carefully designed and controlled hydrogen bomb explosions in deserts to create enormous dust clouds, like huge volcano eruptions do, to cool the earth for two or three years. Then set off more explosions, at intervals. This would give us some time to try to cool the earth more permanently using other strategies. (But what about radioactive dust?)

There are many such proposals for cooling the earth. The point is, though, that they would all take global, governmental cooperation. How can that happen as long

Chapter 17

as capitalists control governments? They couldn't even agree to phase out fossil fuels. Nevertheless, it seems that in terms of saving ourselves and the earth by cooling the earth, especially given the brief time left in which we have to do this, however much we are committed to abolishing capitalism and states, we are stuck with them for now. This is a dismal thought.

Is there a way out of this bind? Remember, if we *could* suddenly abolish capitalism and states (they are thoroughly entwined, one system), we would die, or millions or billions of us would, because the essentials we need to live are currently available only through these institutions (for most of us for most essentials). It would take decades to re-establish an autonomous, self-sufficient existence independent of capitalists and states. We must at least face up to the vast reorganization of social life that would be necessary if we did defeat them.

We must also remember and acknowledge the failure of the three historical strategies for defeating capitalists: (a) seizing the state through elections and using it to destroy capitalists and get to communism (no state/anarchy) -- that is, social democracy; (b) seizing the state with an armed revolution and using the state to destroy capitalists and get to communism (no state/anarchy) -- that is, Leninism; (c) seizing the means of production, establishing workers councils, federating the councils into a dual power structure in order to defeat capitalists, dismantle the state, and get to communism (no state/anarchy) -- that is, anarcho-syndicalism. These strategies did not work, and will not. So it would be a huge mistake to try to rebuild such parties and unions to try again. And besides, even if we did try again, it could not be done soon enough to save the earth. Given the urgency of the situation, however, this does not mean that we should stop asking the existing parties and unions for whatever help they can offer.

So where does this leave us? In dire straits, that's for sure. But where else? We must find ways to weaken capitalists, and their grip on national governments, enough so that the governments, perhaps even with the help of a small minority of capitalists, both under tremendous pressure from below from globally organized citizens, could undertake the massive campaigns needed to cool the earth. Is this even possible? I'm not sure. It doesn't much look like it is.

Perhaps if we consider new and different ways to attack capitalists we could weaken them enough to allow governments to deal with global warming. I'm going to suggest that we shift the focus of anti-capitalist struggles to the entire contemporary international financial system, that is, to *money*: interest, debt, rent, stocks, dividends, stock markets, banks, taxes, but also to where money comes from, who controls it, and its role in the historical evolution of capitalism and its current functioning. Capitalists use money in various ways to enslave us. So if we could take money away from them, perhaps this would be a step toward saving the earth, and toward our own liberation as well.[4]

Interest. Let's start with interest. We could launch a campaign to discredit the very idea of interest and to agitate for its abolition. There is something to build on: the laws against usury in the Middle Ages. Although usury eventually came to refer only to excessive interest, originally it condemned all interest. Isn't it obviously ridiculous that anyone should be able to make *any* money just by loaning money? It is especially ridiculous for governments to borrow money from rich people and then pay interest on it, when they could simply print the money themselves. Yet

---

[4] The two best studies of the international financial system are: Michael Hudson, *Super Imperialism: The Origin and Fundamentals of U.S. World Dominance*. London and New York: Pluto Press, 1972, new edition in 2003, 425 pages; and Michel Chossudovsky, *The Globalisation of Poverty: Impacts of IMF and World Bank Reforms*. London: Zed Books, 1998, 280 pages. Second edition, 2003. For a preliminary bibliography on money in general see James Herod, "Abolishing Money: A Proposed Research Project, with Bibliography," February 2008, at:
   <http://www.jamesherod.info/index.php?sec=blog&id=31>.

Chapter 17

this practice is quite central to capitalism, and has been from its earliest days. Giovanni Arrighi, in his magisterial history of capitalism,[5] demonstrates that from the earliest days of capitalism in northern Italy in the 15th century, rich people helped finance governments -- for a price, of course. Stopping this practice would be a serious blow to capitalists. So we need to be thinking of ways to do this.

We might also consider getting rid of loans as such. Even interest-free loans are still debts, which must be repaid. All wealth is socially created. If it were also socially controlled then communities could decide whether to finance a project or not, and absorb the loss if it didn't pan out. In a cooperative anarchist society, loans, debt, and taxes could be dispensed with completely and forever.

Debt. In recent decades capitalists have enslaved the world with debt (debt peonage) to an extent never seen before -- national debt, mortgage debt, student debt, medical debt, credit card debt, automobile debt, business debt. For a brief period after Occupy Wall Street it looked like an attack on debt might get under way, but it didn't. Yet debt is a great target. It resonates with people.

Debt, along with global warming, are two current crises around which it might be possible to build a massive anti-capitalist movement. These affect everyone. They are global. More and more people should be able to connect the dots between these crises and capitalism. Whole countries are being destroyed by using debt as a weapon.[6]

We could organize debt strikes. Just refuse to repay the loans. If these strikes were massive enough it would seriously harm capitalists and disrupt and undermine their

---

[5] Giovanni Arrighi, *The Long Twentieth Century: Money, Power, and the Origins of Our Times*. London: Verso, 1994, 2nd edition with an added 15-page Postscript, 2010, 416 pages.

[6] See Michael Hudson, *Killing the Host: How Financial Parasites and Debt Destroy the Global Economy*. ISLET-Verlag, 2015, 435 pages. Hudson proposes ten reforms to reign in the financial oligarchy. See Chapter 29, "The Fight for the 21st Century." Two more of his recent books are: *Finance Capitalism and Its Discontents; and The Bubble and Beyond: Fictitious Capital, Debt Deflation, and Global Crisis*.

system.

Rent. Rent is one of the most egregious forms of capitalist exploitation, especially housing rent. I've always been puzzled by the paucity of leftist interest in housing. It is a huge issue for most people, especially those who have to rent. Why would anti-capitalists pay so much attention to the wealth stolen from wage-slaves at work but neglect the wealth stolen from them through housing (owned or rented)? Rent is another great target that affects billions of people. A campaign against rent, including rent strikes, would resonate with them. Such a campaign would involve theoretical and practical attacks on the property laws upon which rent is based.

Stocks, Dividends, Stock Markets. How strange it is, and totally unjustified, that someone can buy a stock (or share) in a corporation and then start receiving dividends without doing anything. It is just money making money. Dividends are the profits from the corporation, that is, the appropriated surplus wealth that has been created by, but seized from, the direct producers. Or most of the profit. A large chunk now goes to bloated salaries for the executive officers. The stocks are traded in stock markets (although a great deal of trading now takes place outside stock markets, in so-called over-the-counter, or off-exchange trading). It shouldn't be hard to discredit these practices and institutions, as immoral, unjust, and exploitative. But this radical critique would need to be infused into an effective strategy for attacking these capitalist oddities. What if thousands of angry protesters occupied the stock markets of the world? What if every shareholder meeting was picketed, occupied, and disrupted, with demands to abolish stocks, dividends, and stock markets? That would be only a start obviously. We'd have to figure out a way to actually dismantle these institutions. At present, anti-capitalists are hardly even broaching this issue. Ultimately, it would mean abolishing property rights, which rest at the core of capitalism. But some intermediate blows to this aspect of

Chapter 17

the system might be found, if we searched for them.

Banks. Banks create money, by making loans, with the interest attached of course. They can be public or private: public, meaning government-owned; private, meaning corporate-owned. In the United States, most banks are private, especially the big banks, including the Federal Reserve Bank. The exceptions are the government-owned Bank of North Dakota, and member-owned cooperative banks and consumer credit unions. Some countries have many cooperative banks, but they are relatively powerless, compared to central banks. We need to focus on the power of the international network of national central banks. They practically run global capitalism. They control the money supply and interest rates. They are enormously destructive. The power of these banks must absolutely be broken.

The European Central Bank is illustrative in this regard. The European Central Bank floats above any national sovereignty. The European Union is not a true federation, with political sovereignty. It is only a monetary union, which adopted a common currency, the Euro, controlled by the European Central Bank. The European Parliament has no power. The EU member states retained political sovereignty but gave up their own national currencies, by adopting the Euro, thus losing control over fiscal policy. It turns out that the establishment of the European Union was a neoliberal capitalist coup. The ECB has been pursuing the current capitalist offensive (neoliberalism) of impoverishing its weaker members (such as Greece) by first indebting them and then seizing their assets to repay the loans, as capitalists have been doing throughout the global south for decades.

The European Union is a special case though. Most central banks are still national banks, although they are networked internationally, and work in tandem with the other big banks to fleece nations. The five biggest US banks, for example -- JP Morgan Chase, Bank of America, Wells Fargo, Citibank, Goldman Sachs -- simply seized the U.S.

Treasury and stole trillions (22, it is estimated) to cover their losses from bad loans, with a little assistance from the Federal Reserve Bank. I saw a sign in an Occupy Wall Street rally: "Give It Back," it read, referring to the trillions of dollars stolen to bailout the banks.

IMF and World Bank. The International Monetary Fund and the World Bank were set up to enslave the weaker nations of the world to debt, and then to strip these nations of their wealth to repay the loans. It has been a fabulously successful strategy and has enormously enriched the ruling classes of the core countries, and also the smaller, local, ruling classes of the targeted nations. These institutions absolutely must be abolished. It is not nearly enough to demand that the unpayable debts be forgiven (a jubilee), or at least reduced to what can be repaid. No, the whole idea of loans with interest must be overthrown and discarded. The trouble is, ruling classes have the power to inflict devastating punishment on any nation which defaults and refuses to pay. But this is the way to go. This is what Greece should have done, what Argentina tried to do but backed off, what Iceland did. Multiple national debt strikes are what is needed to help break the power of the international financial oligarchy -- one of the things. Why aren't anti-capitalists trying to organize such strikes?

Money and Wage-Slavery. Isn't it strange that the money (wage) part of wage-slavery receives so little attention from anti-capitalists? The focus is always mostly on the extraction of surplus value from the workers. Yet from the wage-slave's point of view the wages are certainly of paramount importance. To get money is why they work, in order to buy the necessities for survival.

How did this happen? Capitalists have been destroying relatively self-sufficient peasant societies for centuries, until now, in our times, peasants are approaching extinction. Peasants have been, and are still being, driven off their lands, billions of them over the centuries, and forced to look for jobs, in order to get money, in order to live. They

Chapter 17

were forced to become wage-slaves.

How weird it is actually, and how recent historically, that one has to have a job in order to live. Why isn't this totally unnatural relation under constant attack? Isn't it obvious that in order to escape capitalism the link between jobs and income has to be broken? Why are so many leftists still clamoring for "full employment," which accepts as a given that we have to have jobs to live? Nor are the revived proposals for a "guaranteed annual income" via the government a solution, especially at a time when ruling classes are dismantling the welfare state everywhere.

We could only get out of wage-slavery by shifting to cooperative labor. But we don't have time for that now. I mention this here only to show how central money has been to capitalists, embedded as it is in one of their most essential social creations -- wage-slavery. An attack on money therefore might actually prove to be helpful in abolishing wage-slavery.

Taxes. Taxes are debt. Everyone who is a "citizen" of a state is automatically placed in debt. The state says: "You owe us." This practice goes back to antiquity and to the first formation of states. Taxes are the income of states. You would think that anarchists, at least, who want to abolish states, would have thought a lot about how to deprive states of this income. But they haven't. And now, we need national governments to help cool the earth. I doubt that it could be done without them. So, sadly, anarchy is off the agenda for the time being. After the earth is cooled we can take up our attack on states once again. A fight against taxation might be a part of that struggle.

Corporations. Can we tie in an attack on corporations *per se* to our attack on money? It seems it would be a good idea. Publicly traded corporations issue stocks, pay dividends, typically use credit, and are otherwise integrated into the financial system. What we are dealing with now is a global capitalist ruling class. So why don't we start with the 147 transnational corporations that control 40%

of the global economy.[7] How could we manage to abolish even one of these corporations? We can't seize their factories and offices -- they are scattered all over the world. We can't outlaw them in just one country -- they exist elsewhere. They are wealthier than most small countries. They are defended by the armies of the world. Can we discredit their very existence? We have thousands of anti-capitalist books. Just asking.

So what weapons can we bring to this fight? **(a)** Well, intellectual ones at least. Pound them relentlessly with critiques. Expose their destructive practices. Discredit them. A lot of work has already been done. It needs to be expanded and promoted. We need more media. For these critiques to have a serious impact, however, they would have to be backed by a powerful mass movement, and we don't have that (yet?). Sadly, many of the most prominent global warming activists are not anti-capitalist.

(b) Mass marches and rallies, although 400,000 people marching through New York City on September 21, 2014 in the People's Climate March doesn't seem to have accomplished much. Maybe a lot of people were encouraged to get active. It boosted spirits. We obviously need a lot more than mass demonstrations.

(c) Occupation of buildings. Which ones? Corporate headquarters? Governmental buildings?

(d) Occupation of public squares. That didn't go anywhere, did it?

---

[7] "The network of global corporate control," by Stefania Vitali1, James B. Glattfelder1, and Stefano Battiston, on the web at: <https://arxiv.org/PS_cache/arxiv/pdf/1107/1107.5728v2.pdf>.

Chapter 17

(e) Picketing of persons and corporations. This tactic is often effective in raising awareness and attracting attention to especially egregious offenders of the common good.

(f) Strikes -- debt and rent strikes, everywhere.

(g) Organizations. We have lots of organizations already, dealing with dozens of important issues. They could coalesce into a mass anti-capitalist movement, one which is also linked to cooling the earth, but they aren't, so far: transition towns, new economy movement, slow food, reviving the commons, solidarity economy, organic agriculture, eco-villages, urban gardening, cooperatives, participatory budgeting, permaculture, local currencies, cohousing, clean energy, and so forth. What would it take to radicalize these movements?

Just this brief survey of the left's standard tactics shows how hopelessly inadequate they are for the task at hand. We need more, much more: more militancy, more mass, more organizations, more critiques, more media, more agitation, more strikes, more disruption, more assemblies, more insurgencies, more occupations, more anger. Perhaps if we make a big enough stink we can force some changes. I wish the World Social Forum would become more militant and start concentrating more on global warming.

One good thing: after the Paris climate accords at the Conference of Parties last year (COP 21), the climate justice movement has been moving to organize outside the United Nation's framework, finally. This should have been done after COP 15 in Copenhagen in 2009. But it seems to be getting underway now, thankfully -- a global alliance to try to stop global warming. Perhaps this movement will bypass not only the United Nations but also the United States, which has sabotaged the UN's efforts to deal with climate change from the original Rio treaty in 1992 on down through COPs 1 through 21. Several countries are less hostile to addressing global warming than the United

States. Perhaps the number of such countries will increase.

What I would like to see is a new international anti-capitalist organization that focuses specifically on money, debt, and the entire international financial system, and the oligarchs who run it. It is obscene that the Rothschild family and other historical banking families still have such inordinate power over the peoples of the earth.

This review was published in the **Anarcho Syndicalist Review,** *#69, Winter 2017.*

www.ingramcontent.com/pod-product-compliance
Lightning Source LLC
Chambersburg PA
CBHW061322040426
42444CB00011B/2731